Remember Who You Are

The meditations in this book are available on CD and can be ordered from Infiniti Productions, the audio/visual division of Infiniti Press International 1-800-822-4043.

Remember Who You Are

Insights from the Akashic Records

Shaun Martinz

Infiniti Press International

Infiniti Press International
P.O. Box 294
Chewelah, WA 99109
infinitipress.com
1-800-822-4043

Book design by Poetic Text Publications

ISBN 0-9754863-0-6

Printed in the United States of America

This book is dedicated to those of you who asked the questions so that the rest of us could hear the answers.

Contents

Foreword 3

Introduction to the Akashic Records 5

The Human Experience 9

Karma and Free Will 40

Love and Emotion 70

Plants and Animals 88

The Time/Space Continuum 106

Multidimensional Awareness 123

Ascension 139

Access Your Personal Akashic Records 168

Past Life Meditation 173

The Halls of Records Meditation 188

Invocations to Open the Akashic Records 193

Foreword

Shortly after the events of September 11th, I was guided to begin offering group readings on a monthly basis. The purpose was to gather information to be put into book form to serve as a "guide" for the upcoming quantum leaps in human consciousness. The material presented in this book was channeled through me from the Akashic Records during this series of readings.

Prior to each reading, I was given a topic that was to be the focus of that session, and the people who chose to attend were there to ask the questions that would elicit the most valuable information for those who would be reading the book in the future. In an effort to retain as much as possible of the authentic nature of the information, the text has been edited only for essential grammar, and the result is that the text reads as the dialogue that it was—and is.

When we access the Akashic Records regarding a specific topic, we have access to information about that topic as recorded from the past, present and future. During each session, we were able to draw from our collective human experience of the given subject, and what emerged was essentially an extended conversation with ourselves through time regarding the unprecedented changes that are now occurring.

As I see what has come together in this book, it is amazing to me how timely the information is to the events that are currently taking place. I find it reassuring that our collective guidance had the foresight to present us with such an interesting forum to answer so many of the questions that we are now asking as we move through these extraordinary times.

I feel honored and blessed to be in human form and able to participate in this remarkable transformation, and I eagerly anticipate what we collectively choose to create next.

In Light & Love,
Shaun

Introduction to the Akashic Records

The Akasha is best conceptualized with an understanding of how it interrelates with other aspects of creation. In essence, the Akasha is the fundamental energy at the very core of creation. All that is created emanates from, and returns to, the energy of the Akasha. A recording of the entire human experience on a collective level is held within the Akasha, and information about any issue involving or affecting humans can be accessed through the Akashic Records. There is a recording within the Akasha for virtually all creation, including every person, place and event.

The Akashic Records exist within the Hall of Records and relate solely to the human experience. The Hall of Records is a multidimensional portal into multitudes of realities in which Records of other lineages of Beings that are not human also exist. It is possible to access information pertaining to other lineages and places other than Earth through the Akashic Records, because any time there is interaction with other Beings or interaction in other places involving humans, it is recorded within the Akasha. If a creation interfaces with human experience at any point on the time/space continuum, it is recorded within the Akasha.

The Akashic Records have been in existence since the beginning of this time/space experience and have been referred to in every ancient spiritual teaching throughout history. The Akashic Records have been known as the Cosmic Mind, the Universal Mind, the Collective Consciousness and the Universal Records. In the Bible, they are called "The Book of Life."

Held within the Akasha are the individual records of each soul from the time it leaves its point of origin until its return. At the time a soul makes the decision to experience life as an independent entity, there is a field of energy generated by that experience, and that field of energy is recorded. Every thought, word, emotion and action generated by each soul's experience is recorded within the Akasha. Knowledge on an individual level regarding who each person is, and who he or she is meant to be, is also recorded within the Akasha, and accessing the information from the Akashic Records allows each person to integrate his or her soul purpose into the conscious creation of the individual's reality.

Any time a person participates in any form of creation, it is recorded in his or her personal Akashic Records, as well as in a collective recording of the experience. When questions are asked in group readings, all information that is recorded in the Akasha about that topic from the past, present or future is used to answer the question. It is possible to ask questions about the future and about the past, because the energy of the Akasha exists beyond time/space, where everything occurs in the same moment.

In many cases, what is asked about as a future possibility has already taken place, and as such, the information about that experience is recorded in the Akasha, just as are recordings of those experiences perceived as occurring in the past. Sometimes, possibilities and potentials of a particular experience have not yet occurred, because a decision or choice, on an individual or collective level, has not yet been made. In those situations, information from the Akashic Records can assist in making the pending decisions and choices.

Using questions asked in group sessions, each chapter of this book will offer an aspect of reality from a broader perspective than you may currently perceive it. You will have the opportunity to consider new possibilities through your mind as you read the answers offered by the Akashic Records to questions that will sound familiar, as well as to others that may not have occurred to you yet.

Each chapter also offers a guided meditation that gives you the opportunity to engage more deeply with the new perspectives presented. The meditations offer a way for the information to be assimilated without having to go through your third-dimensional mind. The concepts presented are based on the idea that you are more than your third-dimensional experience, and they will overwhelm your mind, because it has been in the habit of operating third-dimensionally. Doing the meditations will allow you to make quantum leaps in your understanding, because you will be allowing the information to bypass your mind and directly integrate into your creation of reality.

The purpose of this book is to assist you in assimilating the vastness of who you are by expanding your conscious awareness and incorporating a recognition of the perfection in all that you have created. From that place of non-judgment, you will be better able to utilize the information offered as you delve into the Akashic Records. As you remove the obstacles that inhibit your ability to interpret and understand information held within the Akasha, you will be able to consciously access the Akashic Records at any time. Using the information from the Akasha will allow you to create a new reality that encompasses the past and the future, as well as an understanding of the interconnectedness of all consciousness participating in your creation of reality.

Many of the topics presented in this book are presented through the use of comparison. For example, karma and free will, collective consciousness and individual reality, and the third-dimensional human body and the fifth-dimensional etheric body are all discussed in comparison to each other. The reason for the comparisons is that polarity is an essential element of third-dimensional reality, and explanations using comparison and contrast are an effective way of assisting the mind in assimilating the concepts. In some cases, describing what something *isn't* gives us a greater understanding than describing what it *is*, much like negative space can define the outline of an object.

The reason you do not have conscious access to all of the information held within the Akasha at any given moment is because you would be unable to operate under the illusion of separation, and, therefore, would not be able to participate in third-dimensional reality. Essentially, you have set it up so that you will reveal all that you are to whom you imagine yourself to be in the present moment in bits in pieces, so you can more fully enjoy the unveiling of yourself.

Within these pages lies reassurance for your mind that this is, indeed, the time that you have been longing for. As you read the words in this book, your DNA will be activated, and you will bring the hidden wisdom held within your cellular memory out of the archives and into this present moment. It is time to remember how to consciously access the Akashic Records so that you may more completely engage in this time of transition. You cannot fully be of service if you continue to operate under the illusion of forgetfulness, and the Akashic Records hold within them vital experience and knowledge that needs to be incorporated into your consciousness as you awaken. Use the guidance contained in the following pages to reawaken to your true essence and *Remember Who You Are*.

The Human Experience

"So many of you are feeling that you are weary of being human and are ready for ascension."

Are Beings in other dimensions experiencing our human experience from where they are at this time?

Yes, but it is not so much "at this time," because there has always been an awareness of the human experience. It is a very precious, coveted experience to be able to participate in. The reason for that is because it is operating within a time/space constraint, so there is a limited number of Beings that can be here at any given time. We want to talk specifically about the human experience primarily because so many of you are feeling that you are weary of being human and are ready for ascension. We are here to tell you that there are many great things about being human. There are unique aspects to being human that can't be experienced in any other context.

What about the suffering part of the human existence?

That is one of the greatest gifts of being human. We know that you may have difficulty with the term "gift," but suffering can only take place under the illusion that there is separation from all awareness and that everything is not in balance. Part of the reason suffering works so well in this third-dimensional human experience is that you are operating in the illusion of time/space. In reality, everything happens in the same moment. It is all simultaneous. One of the delightful things about being human in a time/space experience is that something uncomfortable can get drawn out for an even longer time.

Just think about how interesting that is from a perspective where everything happens in a moment, where there is no illusion of separation, no experience of density, no understanding of pain, and no comprehension of being separate from. In a time/space illusion, experience can get drawn out so you can get the most out of each phase of it. We are not trying to gloss this over and make it sound like everything about being human is shiny and happy, but we want you to understand that the fact that everything isn't shiny and happy is part of the unique experience of being human—and that is the big attraction! Many of you who are in human form have been doing this for so many lifetimes that you have a great deal of cellular memory and accumulation of what it is like to be human and in separation and in pain. You have been doing it for such a long time that you have become very good at denying your Divinity, and you have forgotten who you truly are, because it seems like such a long time since you have been in wholeness and remembrance. In fact, it has been only a moment—less than a moment.

We want to congratulate each and every one of you on what a good job you have done buying into this game. You have created this, and you have managed to completely forget that you have created it and to feel that the power is not part of yourself. You have no idea how much energy and how much time and how much effort it took you to get to this place. Well done! Congratulations!

You may experience a feeling of melancholy as you begin to rapidly move out of the illusion of being time/space-limited and in density. This will be due to an unconscious awareness of the impending end of the illusion that things move so slowly and seem so dense, and also of the ability to feel emotions so acutely. It can be compared to the feeling of wanting to be with someone that you can't be with, or of wanting to have a job that is not yours, or of wanting anything that you don't have. Desire can only be experienced in a human time/space experience. It is a bittersweet feeling. Many movies and songs often elicit this emotion. As you know, sometimes it is enjoyable to go see a movie where you can cry, or to listen to a song that brings up those feelings. That sense of yearning for something or someone can only be experienced when you are operating under the illusion of separation, and you will feel a loss as you move into awareness and lose the ability to become lost in longing.

On some level, all of you are aware that you cannot be anything other than Divinity. There is no doubt that you are going to end up right back there, and that gives you permission to fully experience the illusion. It can be compared to a wise parent who sets up parameters or boundaries that a child isn't really aware of, and then lets him or her go as far out as he or she can so the child gets the understanding of experiencing different parts of him or herself and pushing those boundaries. Yet, the parent always knows that the child is safe within a contained set of boundaries.

That is how you have set up this experience for yourself. It is not possible to be forgotten, to be left, and to not be able to return to Divinity. That is not even an option. The belief that it is possible allows you to completely dive into the experience and play. It is similar to the way children play within their make-believe stories. They completely buy into them, because they have no fear that it is going to alter the reality that they are in. For them, there is no correlation between the two.

That is part of what is so confusing to you now. It is because you trust yourself so completely that you have given in entirely to this experience and forgotten that it was you who set it up in the first place. Take a minute to remember that you are completely safe, and that you have never been anything other than safe.

Are you telling us to simply enjoy the melancholy and the experience, because we are coming to the end of the time/space continuum?

We are not telling you to do it; we are saying that you are going to start noticing yourself doing it. It won't work to say, "My back really hurts today, so let's enjoy this, because I am not going to be human for much longer." We know that that is not what you are going to do. But, as your vibration increases and the light quotient in your energy field increases, you are going to be less aware of your physicality.

It is going to be like when you start to drift off to sleep, and you relax, because you feel safe about going to sleep. You feel increasingly weightless and not completely in your body. That is going to become more and more the norm. Pain is interesting. When pain is there, you are hyper-focused on a particular part of your body, and that again can only take place in a time/space experience. To be that focused on something slowed down to that extent is unique. So, you may not miss the pain, but you will miss the intenseness of that experience. That is not to say that what you are moving into is not intense, as well, but it is intense in a different way. Being human is a wonderful experience, and so is moving your awareness into the fifth dimension. We are not saying that being human is better than any other experience, but in your mind, you think being human is less than other experiences, and that is not true, either. It is just a different experience.

We like to compare it to different rides at a carnival. Some rides go in circles, some rides go up and down, some rides are a roller coaster, some are in water, and some are on land. They are all simply different ways of experiencing movement. That is all being human is when compared to being in the fifth dimension ,or compared to being in the seventh dimension.

There are unique things about each dimension, and it is important to remember some of the things that you have forgotten about how interesting it is to be human. You have become so deeply involved in them that you have forgotten to think about them as other than as you are. You are not human; you are in human form. There is a difference.

So when we get to the fifth dimension, we won't be human anymore?

Well, let's talk a little about what it means to be human. Humans are kind of the new kids on the block in terms of the timeline we are talking about, because this time/space experience is when humans came into being and expression. What is going to happen now is that humans are going to evolve into the fifth dimension. Many of you have asked about your lineages, and no one has a human lineage, because it hasn't existed before this time/space experience. Keep in mind, of course, that time/space only operates in a third-dimensional experience.

In the future, you will be known as the beginning of a lineage. You are the point of creation of the lineage of humans. If you want to play with this in the timeline continuum model, at some point in the future, someone will ask about his or her lineage, and he or she will be told that their lineage is human, and they will be in awe. It is going to be such an honor. It is something that you are all creating and making up as you go along to pass on to future generations. You had to go through a rigorous screening process to be able to contribute to this new lineage. What a precious, exciting opportunity.

Now we want to make it a little bit bigger. We want you to think about the amount of time involved in what we are talking about. Although this time/space experience has been going on for many, many, many thousands of years, it is but a moment in the whole spectrum of creation. With that being said, humans stand out. When humans are spoken of in galaxies far, far away, everyone knows about the human lineage. Everyone knows what is happening here. This is, in part, because it has never been done before. Those of you in human form are making it up as you go along. No one knows how it is going to turn out. Everyone is sitting on the edge of his or her seat as we move into the fifth dimension, because no one knows what is going to happen. It hasn't been written. Beginning with the fall equinox of 2002, the ten years leading up to 2012 are unknown. There is also an equivalent to that ten-year process once you move into the fifth dimension, but it is not understood in time/space terms, because it will be beyond time/space. The last ten years of the third dimension and the first ten years in the fifth dimension in this birthing process are unknown.

You are going to be a hybrid human or an evolved human: a 3D/5D human. It can be compared to those Beings that populate border towns between different countries, such as Nogales, Arizona or Tijuana, California, where there is a blending of Mexican and American heritages. As Beings move between the third and the fifth dimensions, there will be all kinds of third-dimensional and fifth-dimensional permutations that have not occurred before.

There is a time of choice happening now. We have entered the final months of a three-year window of choice, which will close on the fall equinox of 2002. Each person has been choosing which reality he or she wants to participate in during the final ten years of this time/space experience between 2002 and 2012. Up until this time, the goal has been to gather as much information as possible in the form of life experience. Beings have been looking at what everyone else is doing, and then coming up with their own ideas at the same time to see all the possibilities. Infinite individual and mass consciousness realities have evolved from potential into manifested experiences. It is now time to pull all of those experiences together and decide where you want to go from here. It is useful to imagine this as an hourglass. The available opportunities have been abundant, represented by the expansiveness of the hourglass, and are moving into confluence as humanity moves closer to this time of choice. Options will continue to diminish as you approach 2012. At the same time, the power that is available to humans to create manifested experiences will magnify exponentially. Then, once you move through that portal, available options will expand out again into new experiences of reality.

Keep in mind that what is happening as humans move from the third to the fifth dimension also happens with many lineages between many dimensions. The process of this birthing, or transmutation, is not new, but the players are different. To put this into context, there are other lineages beginning in different places in galaxies far, far away that are as unique and as new as humans are, only in different ways. So, while you are incredibly special and unique, and while this time of transition is noteworthy, know that there are all kinds of incredibly special and unique Beings and events and transitions happening. We want you to try to get your mind around the concept of how special this is, and how natural and normal this is at the same time. Know, too, that many of you who have begun to play with this human lineage are *change agents*, or, as you are known in the cosmos, *transmutation specialists*. This is what you do. That doesn't mean the screening process excludes Beings who have not had the experience, because there is a need for a whole continuum of experience.

We understand that this is just getting bigger and bigger, and we are not trying to overwhelm you, but we do want you to be aware of how many variables you have been juggling and organizing in your cellular body to make this experience happen. It is amazing, and you are all doing so well. The fact that you are all sane and functioning in society is really unique, because in your past lives, it has not always gone this way. The fact that you are not locked up somewhere says a lot about what is different this time. What we are saying is that in past lives, you have played with this idea before. Although it hasn't been the time for this transition between dimensions, some of you were willing to go for it, anyway. Then, someone would lock you up, or burn you at the stake, or cut off your head or something like that. It is all about timing. Because this is a time/space continuum, the concept of timing is important.

Can you talk about the lineages and the planning or the stages that went into creating humans on this planet? What led up to us being here?

It wasn't so much that there was a lack of, as in "we don't have anyone who quite fills this place" as it was, "I wonder what would happen if..." That is an important distinction to be made, because the human race was not to fill anything that was missing; it was to add to everything that already existed. That being said, everything that existed prior to this thought was perfection, just as everything is perfection now that humans exist. We understand that we keep suggesting what appear to be paradoxes, or seemingly contradictory ideas, but we suggest that you just let them move through your mind. They are going to help you get used to thinking less linearly and more multidimensionally, which is the trick right now, because you are still operating primarily third-dimensionally.

It can be compared to when you were playing with little toy people as a young child, and you would put certain people together with certain cars, and in certain buildings or places. It is that kind of creation. The conversation went something like "I wonder what would happen if we put this variable together and this variable together." And someone else said, "Yeah! And then what if we put this in?" And someone else said, "Oh, let's take that one out." That is the seriousness with which this was decided—which is not serious at all. So, stop taking yourselves so seriously. So you are part of the beginning of this tremendously wonderful creative lineage! So what? It is not that big of a deal. At the same time, it is the hottest game in the cosmos at the moment.

So, the human lineage began with a few random ideas and suggestions. The next step was the committees. There are certain committees that assist with proposed creations in this realm. It is like in the third dimension, when you get an idea to build something. Once you formulate the idea, you draw up a proposal and present it to the building committee or the building commissioner or whoever approves the actual construction. Once they approve it, you are able to set the project in motion. That can be compared to the process that the human idea went through.

As the human idea passed through a couple of committees, it began to take on a bit more seriousness. It was recognized that there was more potential than was initially understood. It hadn't occurred to anyone yet to bring potential together in this particular combination. As the excitement began to build around the idea and its potential, the Beings who were involved in the original idea and the Beings who were on the committees continued to contribute suggestions. It is important to keep in mind that everything was done in groups, and they weren't necessarily done in soul groups. It was as if a group of friends, each from different soul groups, came together to launch the project. Part of what was unique about this particular creation and experience was that the Beings who came up with the idea had never thrown all their ideas into the same pot before. It turned out that this group was a really good chemical combination, for lack of a better way of putting it. As the idea went through different committees and continued to generate excitement, it began to be considered as a pilot project for a potential new lineage.

What about this idea that, at certain times in human history, we have been invaded by other E.T. Beings?

We like that word 'invasion,' because it implies a lack of personal power, which is how it played out. When this experiment was set into motion, those Beings participating agreed to specific parameters that would define the experience, and then cloaked themselves in a veil of forgetfulness. Once they moved into forgetfulness, they relinquished control of the experience so that they could experience the illusion of external power. It is the idea that someone has no control over his or her reality that allows the concept of invasion.

The Beings who chose to participate in this experience did not decide that the little green guys were going to come visit on August 2nd. So they were surprised, and that was the fun of it: setting up the potential to be surprised, and then forgetting the possibility. Keep in mind that we are just talking about the human perspective of this experience. There are many other perspectives from those

Beings participating in this experience who are not human. At the time of the first perceived invasion, humans had been in the experience long enough to totally buy into the fact that they were the only Beings around. So when other Beings showed up, it totally surprised them and caused them to reevaluate everything that they thought they were and everything that they thought they had power and control over.

All perceived invasions are within the parameter of the original agreement, but because they take place under the veil of forgetfulness, it is not a conscious agreement. This is relevant, because although this is what a lot of you have personally experienced in your most recent series of lifetimes, it is only now coming into your consciousness. For example, look at the whole idea of being abducted by aliens. If you take the information that we just gave you, it truly is an abduction experience. It truly is an invasion of your experience of who you are, because you have completely forgotten who you are. You are told that nothing can happen to you without your permission, and there is no such thing as being a victim, but it still feels like an invasion. It feels like someone else has more power and more control over your experience than you do. That is how it all fits together. Even while fully engaged in the human experience, you are still operating multidimensionally; you just aren't aware that you are.

So, some things you perpetrate upon yourself, and some things are perpetrated on you by other Beings, who are very good friends of yours and who are only helping you to make this game even more real. It can be compared to a haunted house on Halloween, where you usually know the people or group that put the haunted house together, but you suspend that awareness when you walk through the door because you want the experience of being surprised and frightened. This goes back to the trust element that we talked about earlier. You trust the Beings who put the house together, so you know that no one is really going to cut your head off and that there are no actual dead people. Because you have this element of trust, you can play the game much more authentically and more fully enjoy the experience.

That is what happens when there is a perception of alien invasion or abduction of humans. That doesn't mean that the Beings who are invading you are necessarily your friends, but they have had a conversation with your friends somewhere along the line, and they all know the parameters that define this experience. Regardless of what happens, nothing can take place beyond what you have agreed to participate in.

This is not meant to elicit fear in any way. Experiencing fear is fun. Look at what big business horror movies have become. People will pay a lot of money at the box office to experience fear. If a movie is that much fun, imagine being able to experience an entire reality of it with all your friends contributing to the game. It is great fun!

In the human experience, would it be the personality that is the main thing that keeps one separated from Divinity?

It is not the personality, although the personality is a key component of it. The personality evolves out of the part of you that made the choice to have this experience. The personality is not what is keeping you in separation; it is what is perpetuating separation. So, it is very useful, but doesn't originate there.

It sounds to me like the human experience is about having a great time.

It is all a great drama and doesn't necessarily include only that which you consider negative experience. Consider that being a healer is a participation in the great drama. The whole idea that you can heal another Being is absurd, because each person can heal only himself or herself, but the illusion that one person can heal another works really well in this third-dimensional experience.

There are those who heal and those who want to be healed. It all works out nicely for everyone, because those who are being healed feel like they are getting this great gift and service, and those who are doing the healing feel like they are offering this great gift and service. It is a drama that works for everyone. We are not saying to stop being dramatic. We are saying to notice how good you are at creating drama. You are all drama majors! You know how to create a production so that everyone, even all the people in the production, can get the most out of it. So again, well done!

Is it the separation that makes the drama happen?

The separation makes it possible, yes. Without the separation, the drama wouldn't work, because everyone would see what everyone else was doing at the same time. There has to be that suspension of awareness or knowledge for it to happen.

I wonder, in that sense, how much fun it is going to be to leave the third dimension.

You mean that you are afraid that it won't be as fun as it is here? Now you are starting to get the idea! In reality, it is going to be fun in a whole different way. You have just forgotten how much fun you are having here, and that ties in to what we said before about the melancholy you are going to start to feel. As you begin to remember, which is going to happen quite rapidly, you are also going to recognize that you are remembering. You know that saying, "I wish I didn't know now what I didn't know then"? It is going to be that kind of sensation. That is going to be an in-between period. It may be difficult to understand now, but you will develop a more conscious understanding of what is possible, and that awareness will allow you to move more easily beyond this illusion.

An important thing to be aware of is that there is going to be this kind of back and forth, which you are already seeing in your life. For a day or two, you will feel as if you are in sync. Everything will be flowing, and everything will be going great. Then, for the next few days, it seems like everything goes to hell. Your timing is off, everything feels wrong, and you wonder, "What just happened?" You will go back and forth like that, and you will do that because you still want to play in this third-dimensional illusion. You are beginning to want to remember what it is like to be out of the third dimension, but you are not quite ready to completely let go. You will begin to notice that every time you pull yourself back into the third dimension, you are able to pull yourself out more quickly, and you don't buy into it as deeply. But you are not yet ready to stop buying into it entirely, and that is okay.

When you find yourself in a seemingly familiar situation, don't throw up your hands and say, "I am back to square one!" At this point, you can't go back to square one. Square one is not as interesting to you anymore. You are in a spiral, not in a circle. Think about that image. When you find yourself in a familiar situation, know that even though it feels the same, it isn't. You have learned and changed so much that you have forgotten everything that you have learned and that has changed since the last time you were a similar place. Remember, always come back to trust. Trust yourself. Trust that as much fun as the third dimension is, you have committed to moving into the fifth dimension. You are on your way. A part of you is keeping an eye on you, and it won't let you go backwards. It won't let you return to the same relationships, to the same job, to the same lack of financial resources. All of these things that are creating the illusion of lack or separation are going away.

So, what is happening is like a play? We have already been through the first act, we are now in the second act, and we already know what's going to happen in the third act?

Yes and no. That is a good linear way to think about it. At the same time—not in place of—think of the fact that you are also playing the first act over again in different ways. You play all the way through the first act and think, "That was interesting. I want to go do it again." Then, you switch a few things, and go back to do it again. That is why you know what comes next, because you have already been there fifteen times. That is not to say that what you said about moving from the first act to the second act to the third act isn't true, as well.

I think of my children playing. When they play a game, they go back and play it again and again...

Good example. They go back and make up new rules each time based on what happened the last time. Exactly. In fact, you are doing both at the same time. Part of you keeps playing out the first act, and another part of you is moving on. The part of you that is in act four is sending information back to the part of you that is performing the first act over and over again, and that information changes how you perform act one.

Are all people involved in this transmutation, or only a certain segment of the people on Earth?

All Beings on Earth are involved in a choice, because Earth herself is going to stop being third-dimensional in 2012, but not all Beings are interested in moving into the fifth dimension. There is a whole continuum of choices available. One choice is to move from the third dimension to the fifth dimension and to participate in a fifth-dimensional illusion of reality for a time. It is another possibility to choose to move in and out of the third and fifth dimensions, to consciously go back and forth. This option is not going to be like what we talked about earlier, where you create flow and movement one moment, and then you create frustration, pain and confusion the next. Instead, it is going to be the best of both worlds. It will be like a "Greatest Hits" collection of music. You get the greatest hits of both the third and the fifth dimensions, and you can play them over and over again with different variations.

An interesting aspect of the choice to move between the third and the fifth dimensions is that you can experience yourself as a 3D/5D hybrid human, while still participating in the third dimension. As a hybrid human, you will have a different perspective than you do now as you interact with other Beings who still perceive themselves as only third-dimensionally human. Remember that all Beings are at different stages in their process. Many of the Beings that you call masters, teachers and guides are choosing to move into another experience, and those Beings that choose the hybrid human experience will become the new masters, teachers and guides.

From the perspective of a hybrid human, it is possible to see the vibrational and energetic fields of other Beings and observe when those fields change. At this point, you can't even imagine what that is like. Those of you who are healers have a sense of when someone's energy comes into balance or when something shifts for them, but from a hybrid human perspective, there is so much more. It is a color, it is a sound, it is a vibration, and it is amazing to watch someone transform before your very eyes. Beings are inspired to change merely by being in the presence of a hybrid human. It is not an inevitable duty or responsibility to evolve into a hybrid human and assist others; it is merely one of the many choices available in this time of transition. It is also an option to move out of the third dimension and beyond the concept of dimensionality entirely. At the other end of the spectrum, it is also possible to continue to experience the third-dimensional reality.

Beings who make the choice to continue to experience the third dimension are going to be provided with another opportunity, another planet, or another place to do so. It is not as if all Beings who make that choice will have the same experience. There are a multitude of possibilities of how that choice can play out. For those Beings who want to continue to experience a third-dimensional illusion of reality, it will be as if they wake up one morning on a different planet that is not Earth. They will have a vague memory of Earth for a little while, similar to the way you might remember part of a dream, and then they will forget about it. It will be as if they have been in the new experience the whole time, because the part of them that is aware of the game they are playing wants to help them stay in the illusion.

We understand that it might be difficult for you to understand why anyone would choose to continue to experience a third-dimensional reality, but keep in mind that those of you in this room have participated in this time/space experience from the beginning. Many Beings who are still interested in the third-dimensional experience came in halfway or three-quarters of the way through, and they haven't had their fill of the third dimension yet.

What do you consider the third dimension?

Third dimension is density, in the sense of physical solidness. It is time/space. Third dimension is the illusion of separation. Speaking in words is very third-dimensional. So much is lost when you use words, which serves the third-dimensional idea of separation very well. Because there is so much that is not said, it is great fertile ground for misunderstanding, division and misinterpretation. It can be compared to when you watch soap operas. In soap operas, someone is always lying to someone else, and it always catches up with him or her, and then there is all this drama that plays out. That is an example of an experience that you could only have in a third-dimensional reality. War is also a solely third-dimensional experience. In a third-dimensional illusion of separation, there is not only the possibility of misunderstanding between individuals but also of misunderstanding between groups of individuals.

You said something a minute ago about going between the third and fifth dimensions, but that the third dimension will not be on the planet Earth?

It will not be on Earth, because Earth is going to be in the fifth dimension. There will be places, possibilities and planets in which to experience third-dimensional realities. Earth no longer wants to express herself as a third-dimensional Being, but there are others who would like to experience themselves third-dimensionally. Consider the possibility that you could experience yourself as a third-dimensional planet. Think about this, with the different options that we have laid out. There have to be all kinds of Beings to play out the dramas or the plays of all these illusions of reality. So, someone gets to be the planet. Think how much fun it would be to be a planet!

Is any of this already designated in contract? Did we already decide this, or can we change the game?

Yes, to both of those questions. Some Beings knew that they wanted to move beyond the third dimension, but they weren't sure how they would feel when they reached this time of transition, so they left a few options open. They knew that the options included being a planet, a star, a fifth-dimensional human, a hybrid human, or even a multidimensional cat, but they wanted to wait until the fall equinox of 2002 to make the actual choice. Other Beings didn't have any idea which direction they wanted to move in, and those Beings kept all options open, including not moving beyond the third dimension at this time of transition. There were also Beings who knew exactly what they wanted to do, and that is what they are choosing, as well as Beings who thought they knew, but are now altering their choices. It has a lot to do with how much previous experience Beings have had with times of transformation. We suggest that you think of contracts as agreements that are not written in stone and that can always be changed.

Many things have happened in this time/space experience that were unprecedented, and these unexpected events have an impact on the decisions that are being made now. Some people have known for the last two years exactly where they are supposed to live and exactly what they are supposed to be doing. Others are getting closer and closer to knowing as they keep making choices, and inherently eliminating other choices. And there are still others who perceive so many possibilities and options that they can't make any decisions. For those people, this is a really uncomfortable time. Not choosing might be making them sick, extremely stressed out, or even depressed.

Having difficulty making choices is an important thing to talk about. You resist deciding because of the finality of what that means, either consciously or subconsciously. It feels like once you choose, that is it. A part of you knows that you are never going to be at this moment of choice again. You worry that you are never going to have opportunities like this again. You are having a hard time deciding what to let go of, because all possible experiences are appealing on some level. So, what we would like to tell you is to go ahead and choose something. Once you experience that reality for a few days, weeks or months, you will know if that is a direction you want to continue in. The thing that you are forgetting is that if you decide that you would prefer another direction, you can always re-choose. Let up on the pressure a little, and that will actually help you make a choice. Although it is true that you are never going to be in this exact moment again with these exact same choices, there are going to be other opportunities to choose from a whole different set of possibilities. It is okay to let something go. You will actually feel much better once you do make a choice. It is the constantly trying to decide that is wearing on you.

Just make a decision already! You may know immediately if it is the wrong decision, and you can reverse it, or you might know in a couple of weeks or a couple of days, but make a decision—any decision. Not deciding is manifesting in headaches and pain in your neck and lower back. Go ahead and make some decisions. We are not saying to try to trick yourself by making a decision you don't really mean to follow through on. You need to be truly committed to making a decision. For example, maybe your job is making you crazy. You really hate it. Decide at dinner one night that you are going to quit your job. Remember to really make the decision. This is important to clarify, because some people quit every night at dinner, and then they go back to work the next day. We will give you a meditation to help you with this.

Call to mind some of the issues that you are having difficulty making decisions about. Now, choose one of those issues, and imagine definitively making up your mind one way or another. Consider all of the actions that would be required to commit to that decision. For example, if you are thinking about quitting your job, envision telling your boss that you are quitting. Or, if you are considering moving into a different house, envision calling a realtor and putting your house on the market. You might choose to finally go put the down payment on that art studio you have wanted to lease, or submit an article to a magazine that you have been putting off, or register for the class that will give you the certification you need to move into a new line of work. It can be any one of the many choices that you are currently struggling with.

Once you decide which scenario you want to focus on, play it out in your mind detail by detail. The first step is to imagine taking the action. The second step is to notify all the people involved. The third step is to tell a few people about what you have done. You can envision calling someone on the phone, sending out an email, or visiting someone and telling him or her about what you have done. Imagine how the conversation might go.

Once you have completely played out all three steps of the scenario, including making the decision, taking the appropriate actions, and telling a few people about it, it is time to let it go. You can do this in whatever way occurs to you. For example, see yourself washing your hands, and know that you are washing your hands of any further worry or concern. Then, see yourself drying your hands, and know that you have faith in the outcome of what you have decided. Or, see your decision written on a chalkboard, and see yourself taking an eraser and completely erasing the words, knowing that you are erasing any further worry or concern. Then, see yourself walking way from the chalkboard, and know that you have faith in the outcome of what you have decided. You can play this out in myriad ways; be creative.

You might experience some emotion, but it may not be the emotion that you expect. As you play out the scenario in your mind, you might be surprised to find that you feel calm and confident, instead of frustrated and angry. It is not necessary to consciously attempt to control your emotions, but just notice how it does play out without any judgment. Take a few minutes now, and do this meditation...

☸

The reason that this meditation is useful is because it will give you the opportunity to experience your choices in a way other than through your mind. Because you are moving out of the time/space experience, and you are moving out of linear, logical decision-making, trying to make these decisions in a linear, logical way is just not working for you anymore. That is why you are so frustrated. Put your habitual ways of making decisions aside. Try this meditation, and it will become clear what you are meant to do. Expect to know what you are meant to do, and you will. You actually already do know. Your mind is just getting in the way.

Remember to not be afraid to make a choice and to take an action. Part of your fear exists because you are still operating in time/space. Essentially, while operating in a time/space reality, you have to let go of one thing to allow something else to come in. You need to trust that you will not be left hanging. It is like a cartoon where someone runs off the cliff, and they are just standing out in space for a while before they realize that they no longer have solid ground beneath them. We understand that that is what it feels like we have been asking you to do. In reality, we are there with open arms to catch you, but you have forgotten that.

Try to come at it from a different angle. Consider the possibility that your mind doesn't have to make this decision. Remember that there is a part of you that knows what is going on here. You are safe. You can trust that you are going to end up where you are supposed to be, despite your best intentions to mess up any sort of plan that another aspect of yourself has set into motion. Don't be afraid to make some decisions and take some action. That is how this meditation is helpful. When you allow your mind to explore the possibilities more fully, you give it a little bit more information to deal with, and in doing so, the various options may feel less threatening.

When you do this meditation on your own, it can take five minutes, a half-hour, or as long as you want. The time involved isn't important. As with all of the meditations we give you, you don't have to go sit in a room in lotus style and light up the incense. This can be something that you do while you go for a walk, while you do the dishes, or as you are drifting off to sleep. We don't suggest you do it when you are driving to work if your issue is with work, or while you are fighting with your partner if your issue is with him or her. We suggest that you make a conscious effort to incorporate what you do multidimensionally into more of your daily life, being careful to choose the times that you do this. The goal is to expand your conscious awareness, not to escape your conscious reality. This will help you get used to the idea of being human and hybrid human at the same time.

I read something recently that said that whenever we set something into motion in non-physicality, we are in fact creating a parallel reality where that is actually happening. Is that true?

What happens is that you move out of a singular time/space-limited reality. It is as if you experience a simultaneous reality while this reality gets put on hold. It is like what happens in the book *The Lion, The Witch and The Wardrobe* (Lewis, 1950), when the children go into the wardrobe and experience an entirely different reality in which years go by. Yet, when they come back through the wardrobe, they have only been gone for a matter of minutes. It is like that. Any time that you set something new into motion, you create the possibility of a variety of simultaneous experiences, and then you choose one of them to consciously participate in.

I find that I come across new things in my life, and all of a sudden, I'm really passionate about this new thing, and I focus all of my creative energy into it. It can go on for a couple of days or a couple of weeks, and all of a sudden, it is just done, before it ever becomes physicality. Is that being created on another level?

That is what we were talking about a minute ago. You made a choice, and you just went for it. It then either played itself out, or there was a different direction you were meant to go when you made the decision. That is an example of what we were saying. You can totally throw yourself into something, and you are not going to get yourself backed into a corner or create a mess that you will have to clean up. That is exactly what we were talking about.

Any time you make a choice and take action, you gather more information and are presented with the opportunity to choose again. Sometimes the experience that you choose is needed to provide you with another piece of the puzzle, and sometimes it is simply something you want to experience, for whatever reason. Remember, none of these decisions are that big of a deal. They are not about life or death, even if it feels that way. It may feel like your financial energy or your mental health is dependent on them, as well as the roof over your head or having enough food to eat. But it truly is not that dire. All you have to do is follow your heart, and all those issues that you are so worried about will resolve themselves.

You must learn to trust yourself. Trust the idea that if something catches your attention or occurs to you, that it is yours to do. You must learn to differentiate between the kinds of fear that you experience when presented with a choice. Begin to notice the difference between the part of you that says, "That is not where I am supposed to go," and the part of you that says, "That is exactly where I am supposed to go, but it looks scary." When you know it is the right choice to make, but it still feels scary, envision in your mind another part of yourself forging the path and shining a flashlight on the path ahead of you, or envision the multidimensional aspects of yourself lined up along the path ahead of you. You can visualize one Being, or a multitude of Beings, or anything in between, and know that those Beings are other parts of yourself or good friends of yours in another dimensional reality, and that they are going to help you get to where you need to go.

Another fact to take into account is that the time/space experience isn't as concrete as it used to be. That means you can play with changing your reality right in the middle of experiencing a different reality. Think about how, in a dream, you might find yourself doing something, and as soon as you think, "I don't want to do this," you can just stop doing it. Consider the possibility that you could do the same thing in the middle of a reality that you are experiencing while you are awake. If you make a choice and it takes you in a direction that you don't like so much, begin to look for an opportunity for it to change. Be open to the possibility that it can completely change in an instant. Other Beings can change, or the opportunities available to you can change. It can change to something that feels more comfortable to you in that moment, right in the middle of the experience. Let go of the idea that everything has to be played out completely anymore. Things just aren't that concrete. Begin to perceive your waking reality, and to interact with your waking reality, as you do in your dreams.

Do this in small ways at first, with issues that don't carry a lot of emotional attachment for you. For example, don't begin changing realities that affect your financial energy or your home or people who are important to you. Start with little things, like what you are going to wear in the morning, or how you interact while driving in traffic. Notice what you are doing and what other drivers are doing, pay attention to the choices that you make and the consequences of those choices, and play with changing the choices and/or changing the consequences, just as you would if you were dreaming. Of course, don't set yourself up in dangerous ways. Maybe you are in the grocery store, and you are about to crash into someone with your cart. Set the intention that you don't want to crash into him or her, and watch to see what happens to intervene. You don't have to do anything, just set the intention.

Your linear mind doesn't have to figure out what is going to happen, because the possibilities that it will consider will be too limiting. What will happen is that those Beings whose job it is to create this perpetuation of reality for you will have a quick meeting, decide what to do, and in a split second, they choose the most interesting option for you. Begin to do this any time it occurs to you. As you gradually see that it works every time—which it will—you can begin to do it in areas of your life that carry more weight. It is simply a matter of regaining that trust in yourself.

If we have that much ability to control this reality, why do some of us stay in diseased states, or why do we get sick, and why can't we change that? If we do have this power to create and to not create, then what is it that is making us stay in a reality of disease?

You continue to manifest a disease state because you are still getting something out of creating that reality. There is still something in it for you. Consider the possibility that if you become completely whole, healthy and balanced, you are likely to immediately ascend, and you are not quite ready to do that yet. Because part of you knows this, you are kind of over-compensating. You don't want to take the chance of getting that close to ascension, because you are not ready to leave this experience yet. To ensure that you don't leave too soon, you are taking it a little to the extreme at this point.

There are actually two questions here, because there are two different approaches to how this is happening. The first perspective is held by people who are aware that they can heal themselves and be whole, yet still continue to manifest discomfort or disease. Those Beings are manifesting their reality based on their cellular memory of what it takes to stay here in the third-dimensional experience at this time, knowing on some level that it wouldn't take much to leave. The veil is thinning, and it is quite possible that you are just staying anchored in because you really like it here and aren't ready to leave just yet. For those of you who feel like this, begin to notice what it is you love about being here and about being human. That will create the opportunity for you to stop creating such intense ways of staying here, and will allow you to remain here without needing to create physical discomfort to keep you grounded.

Now, let's talk about the other option. Beings who are not really interested in leaving the third dimension and are creating disease, are doing so because they are still perpetuating their illusion of third-dimensional reality. They don't have any intention of leaving yet, because they are still in the middle of experiencing physicality, not at the end, like you are. For those Beings who want to move out of the third dimension but are still manifesting disease, it can be really frustrating, because they have the awareness and know that it can be different. And it is especially frustrating when it is not the way that they know it can be. This is an instance of overreaction. It is a matter of what is literally being manifested in their bodies. When a disease begins, it is a body's attempt at correcting something that is out of balance. If it stays out of balance, the body continues to correct, and eventually goes too far off balance to maintain physicality. Those Beings who are still in the troughs of third-dimensional reality will eventually die, while those Beings who are becoming multidimensional will eventually return to balance. It is necessary to begin to recognize the things that are enjoyable about being in the third dimension at this time to bring your body into balance, and doing so will eliminate the need to create disease and discomfort to stay here.

I'm becoming pretty good at making these day-by-day choices about what feels good and what doesn't. The part that I struggle with is the recognition of different aspects of myself, higher layers of who I am who will step in sometimes and take over and remind me that I can relax, that I don't have to worry about this drama or something else. The choice I'm trying to make is to stay in that higher consciousness, and I keep getting knocked back out of it. It is like I can't quite fully make that choice, even though I desperately seem to want to. It seems to not be fully available to me.

That is happening for many Beings. The reason is that you actually don't want to make that choice yet. We understand that it might feel confusing, but it is the same thing that we were talking about with the question that was just asked. Begin to recognize how interesting it is when you are denying these higher aspects of yourself, and then the need to do it will ease. Appreciate the last vestiges of time that you have in this third-dimensional experience, and at the same time, continue to nourish and support the desire you have to move beyond this dimension, because that is what is propelling you forward. Actually, don't think of it so much as moving forward, but more as a plant or flower coming into bloom.

As your appreciation of the third dimension increases, your movement into the fifth dimension will be enhanced. This is a hard concept to understand, because you are still operating in linear time, but there is a direct correlation here. You can only ascend by fully descending. Many of you have achieved an extreme point of descension and density, and it has become quite uncomfortable. We always talk about being grounded and this is what we mean: be here, be fully present here on the Earth. Let yourself completely descend, and that will allow ascension to make more sense from a cellular perspective, which will then translate into a mental perspective.

So, be more present in this third-dimensional experience. Look at the good things about the job that you don't like. Look at the good things about the place you currently live and that it is time for you to move away from. Many of you are in major transitions at this time, and that is the force that we are talking about, the momentum that is moving you forward. Remember the reason that you took the job you currently have. Remember why you live in your present home. Whatever you are experiencing, at some point there was a reason that you made that choice. Things may have changed, but it is important to remember why you made that original decision. Stop beating yourself up about the fact that you are in your present situation, and appreciate the fact that you created it. That, in and of itself, will allow you to begin letting go of your attachment to perpetuating the experience.

You can't trick yourself by saying, "Okay, I moved in here because it has really great hardwood floors," and then immediately begin to focus on how much you now hate to polish those same floors. You have to remember what it felt like the first time you walked into that house and fell in love with it. Remember how excited you felt when you walked out of that interview and knew that you had snagged that job. In relationships, remember what you liked about that person in the beginning, and look for it again. Even though whatever drew you into a particular experience may not be there in the current moment, remember why you initially chose it. By calling those memories to mind, you will begin to rediscover trust and honor in what is yours to do.

You have not made any mistakes here. It is only from a third-dimensional perspective that this experience has been about learning lessons. In actuality, it has never been about reaching a certain level of awareness that would allow you to ascend, because you have had access to that information all along. You just wanted to experience what it felt like to imagine that you didn't. In truth, you could have left at any moment, and instead, you chose to stay, because it is a really interesting experience. When you think about it from that perspective, it changes everything, and allows you to move from feeling powerless to claiming your divinity.

The melancholy time that you have been talking about, could you elaborate on it? Is it more of a feeling or an attitude?

It is a feeling, and it comes and goes. It is a fleeting feeling, and it may not even be associated with anything that is going on at the moment. You may just suddenly feel kind of melancholy. We don't want to quite say sad, because it is not sad. It can feel like depression, which is an important thing to know. There might be some days when you just don't want to get out of bed. The day just doesn't seem interesting. Or, perhaps you will suddenly have the feeling that something that used to be part of your life is gone, and not even know what it is, exactly. Sometimes you may attribute it to the song on the radio or the movie you are watching, but it doesn't always have that direct correlation. The reason it happens like this is because you are not as linear and as encapsulated in time/space as you used to be. You are making a decision about something that you are not consciously aware you are experiencing in a given moment. The melancholy is because you are letting go of something that you may not even be consciously aware of.

That is actually a much more effective, efficient way of moving through this time, because you don't have to run everything through your mind. While your mind is busy focusing on the reality that appears to be right in front of you, you are, at the same time, making a multitude of decisions that are moving you closer to ascension. Many times, the unconscious decisions being made were set into motion by meditations or things that you have done in the dream state that are moving through your awareness in a time/space moment. That is a good example of something to appreciate about the 3-D experience: being aware that everything is slowed down to such an extent that you see everything more clearly as it is happening. It can be compared to how you might hold an insect in your hand and closely examine every intricate detail about it and treasure it. That degree of analysis can only happen in a third-dimensional experience, because outside of a time/space dimension, everything happens simultaneously. It is this simultaneous awareness of what is happening consciously, unconsciously, and multidimensionally that you are stepping back into.

Is the melancholy state also a transitional period, kind of like moving from the third dimension to the fifth dimension?

That is what the melancholy is about, yes. Once you move past this, you can come back into the third dimension, but you can never come back into the third dimension in the way you are here now.

You will never be again in this exact time, operating under this same level of illusion of separation. The melancholy is directly related to that awareness. We keep reassuring you that you are doing a good job, but part of you already knows what a good job you have done, and that is where the melancholy comes in, too. You are choosing to move away from a creation that you have put a lot of time and effort into.

The other thing to remember as you move into the fifth dimension is that everything that you have experienced here is going to be retained in your cellular memory. You will retain access to everything that has happened here, but it is not going to be as interesting from that perspective as it is now. That, too, is part of the melancholy, the awareness that the things that are so precious to you now are never going to feel this dear again, because they are going to be in a different context. It is not better or worse; it is just different. So, begin to appreciate the preciousness of the bittersweet feeling of leaving one experience for another, because it cannot be experienced in the same way from a fifth-dimensional perspective.

Can you describe what the fifth dimension is like?

The most useful way to describe it is in contrast to the third dimension. Did anyone feel a little dizzy or a little bit disoriented just now? We gave you that feeling as a little taste of the fifth dimension—at least how the fifth dimension feels from a third-dimensional perspective. It is not as tangible, you are not as tangible, and reality itself is not as tangible. Telepathy is an example of fifth-dimensional communication. Another example is described in the book, *The Secret of Shambhala* (Redfield, 2001), the third book in *The Celestine Prophesy* series. The homes that they live in exist multidimensionally, so if they perceive that they are in danger, they do not allow them to be perceived third-dimensionally. It might be an interesting book for you to read to help you better understand the fifth dimension.

In the fifth dimension, there still is a degree of separation of Beings. It is not as if everyone returns to one mass consciousness or group consciousness, but there is more awareness between Beings of what is going on with other Beings. There are conflicts originating from widespread misunderstanding, like war. If any of you have retained, or are aware of, any Atlantean memories, it is more like that. Food is lighter, although food in the form that you consume in the third dimension isn't necessary. In the fifth dimension, there is still separation from the source where nutrients or energy feeding come from. When you are in the fifth dimension, you can go out in your front yard and stand in the sunshine for five minutes, and that recharges you. It feeds you. It is an energy exchange that happens between the elements, but in a different way than in the third dimension.

There is also that kind of exchange between Beings. There's not sex, per se, in the fifth dimension, but there is an energetic exchange that is exponentially more enjoyable than sex. But it is different. That is not to diminish sex in the third dimension, because sex in the third dimension is very physical and very concrete and between two very separate bodies. In the fifth dimension, it is more of an energetic exchange. There is a similar exchange between parents and children, as well. Because of this, there is not the typical breakdown in communication between parents and children during the teenage years that is common in the third dimension.

Hopefully that begins to give you a feel for the fifth dimension. There is still separation, but it is a different kind of separation, and there is much more conscious awareness of the other when it does exist. These are the kinds of things that you are going to start playing with in the next few years. You will also have the option to immediately move fully into a fifth-dimensional reality, but it is interesting to not do it so quickly, so you can experience the differences between the two dimensions.

Are we becoming like the lady in Australia who is a breatharian?

Yes, that is an option in this third-dimensional experience. Being a breatharian is not a purely third-dimensional experience; it is the fifth-dimensional experience happening in the third-dimensional realm. It is a fifth-dimensional technology, if you will, but she is experiencing it in the third-dimensional realm. Telepathy, teleportation, animal communication, conscious manifestation of reality, conscious awareness of multiple realities, conscious creating, and simultaneous manifestation are all fifth-dimensional technologies. Although creation and manifestation are actually simultaneous, in the third dimension you can experience them as two different things.

If you want to play around with what the fifth dimension feels like, when you are drifting off to sleep you can ask to have a fifth-dimensional experience and remember it. In the beginning, you may not remember the experience in detail, but you will retain a distinctly different feeling when you wake up. You can also try it when you are awake. Ask to experience the current moment from the fifth-dimensional perspective, and then notice how you feel. The key to understanding the fifth-dimensional consciousness is to pay more attention to how you feel in any given moment.

As we said earlier, we suggest that you begin to consciously play with non-linear, fifth-dimensional experiences while in the middle of a third-dimensional experience. Remember not to start with issues that elicit strong emotions for you. Begin with aspects of your life that you don't have a lot of emotions around, or attachments to, so you can see a few times that it works. That will allow you to get the hang of it. This is something that you already know how to do and that is innately a part of you, so you just need to remember what it feels like by playing with it every chance you get.

Is paying attention to our dreams and the symbolism in our dream state a way of bringing the fifth dimension into the third dimension?

Yes. The fifth dimension is already here, and you are becoming more aware of it. We would actually encourage you to go one step further and become more engaged with it by actively participating in your dreams. We don't mean keeping dream journals or anything that tedious, necessarily—maybe it is not tedious for everyone—but we are trying to make this easy and light. Just play with consciously altering what happens in your dreams. It will also help you to play with consciously altering that which you call daily reality as if you were in the dream state. It isn't that big of a leap, and now is the time to blend your waking and dreaming realities, which is the same thing as moving between the fifth and third dimensions.

Could you give a few more examples of how we would play with reality during the waking state as if we were in the fifth dimension?

Another example could be while you are having a conversation with someone. Again, don't do this during a conversation with someone with whom you have a lot of baggage. It won't work. Maybe when you are talking with someone at work over the water cooler, you could expect him or her to say something other than what would make sense in the conversation. Another thing to take into account is that when that happens, and reality shifts like that, everything instantly shifts around it to make it seem normal. So, you might notice in the moment that it happens that something is out of place, but in a split second, you will begin to participate in the new conversation and perpetuate the reality that you just shifted into. That is your mind's job: to make sense of your reality. Consider being less attached to things making sense all of the time, and you will begin to become more aware of the fifth-dimensional perspective in your everyday reality.

Here is another example. At some point during the day, you can entertain the thought that you are wearing something different than what you put on earlier that morning. Become aware that you are wearing something different but you don't know what it is. Then look down at yourself to see what is different. We want to let you know that your mind is going to have a really hard time with this. You may notice that your socks are a different color, but then you are going to suddenly remember that, although you originally put on the blue socks, you went back later and changed into the green socks. That is okay. Let yourself play that scenario out, and at the same time, recognize that reality is shifting behind you to change into the reality you just created.

Have fun with this. Don't take it all so seriously. Just play with these different perspectives. None of this is real, anyway. That is why it is called an illusion of reality. It is just a big game, or a series of games, from a third-dimensional perspective, and a multitude of simultaneous games from the fifth-dimensional perspective.

When an adult is trying to teach a young child that things that are out of sight are not really gone, he or she first takes a toy out of sight, and then pulls it back into view to demonstrate that it has not permanently disappeared. Play those kinds of games with yourself, only do it in the opposite way. Consider the possibility that matter can change form. Place something in front of yourself, maybe a shape of a square, and watch it change into a star in your mind. Eventually, you are going to be able to do this in actual physicality. In the not-too-distant future, you are going to be able to do this with tangible objects. But first, you have to remember what it feels like, and visualizing it happening is a good place to begin.

Have the same patience and understanding with yourself as you would with a child. Sometimes, when you show a child a toy, and then take it away and bring it back, the child completely forgets about it and contentedly goes on to something else. You know that it is not a big deal, because the child has the rest of his or her life to figure it out. Treat yourself with that same kind of understanding. You don't have to meditate or affirm into infinity until you get this. You don't have to insist that you are not going to do anything else until you get this concept. That is just not going to work, just as it doesn't work with a child. If you insist, the child becomes more and more frustrated, just as you become more and more frustrated with yourself, because you are not getting it, and you think you should. If you aren't getting it, it just means that there is something else that is more interesting to you at the moment.

To continue with our child example, sometimes he or she just wants to go outside and play in the backyard and really doesn't care about what you are trying to show him or her. When you aren't making any progress with what you have been focusing on, even though it may be a really good concept, go do something else for a while. Either you will come back to it with complete understanding, or it won't be relevant anymore.

Be patient and gentle with yourself, because you have all the time in the world. That is actually quite funny, because that is all the time there is left in this world, literally. Time/space is irrelevant. There is no need to feel that anything has to be done by any certain time, or to worry that if you don't get something done by a certain time, there are going to be consequences in terms of your physical body or your relationship or your job. Reassure yourself that you have all the time in the world to make a decision. Then, make a decision, and see what happens. Take action, and don't be immobilized by a feeling of responsibility or heaviness. That is another fifth-dimensional idea that you can start playing with right now: that things are already lighter, because, in truth, they are. Feel yourself lightening up. Do you feel the weight on your shoulders? Okay, maybe you don't want to completely give it up, but just raise it a little bit, so that it hovers just above your shoulders. Practice allowing all the weight of your life to hover just above your shoulders. How fifth-dimensional is that? It is like a backpack that you carry around, but don't actually wear.

We are giving you some very rudimentary ideas. You are the humans. You are the ones that can come up with the creative ways to move into the fifth dimension. We are looking to you, so when future groups ascend, we will be able to share with them what you have learned. We will put it in a handbook for them. You are the pilot project, remember?

You are represented on a multitude of levels. We will talk more about that when we talk about multidimensional awareness, but before we move into that, we want you to have a good grasp of what it is to be human. With a clear understanding of the uniqueness of being human, you won't forget the power of being human when we move into a multidimensional awareness. It is very important that you carry your humanness with you when you move into the experience of multidimensional awareness. We honor the human expression that all of you are, and we would like, more than anything, for you to remember how wonderful it is that you are human.

Karma and Free Will

"When you are operating karmically, you are not present in the now."

Why are karma and free will in the same talk? How are they linked together?

Karma and free will are different aspects of the same concept. Karma is understood to mean that when you take an action or make a choice, there is a reaction or consequence as a result of that action or choice. Karma can occur within a lifetime or can be carried through multiple lifetimes. It can take place within an instant or over millennia. It is important to remember that Earth, in this time/space continuum, exists as a free will zone, and karma allows you to more fully experience free will. Karma is simply a creation used to experience the third-dimensional components of time and space.

Essentially, when you are working with karma, you are experiencing your free will, and the free will of others, slowed down. It can be compared to how animation is created by moving a series of pictures really fast, one after another, to create the illusion of movement. It is useful to conceptualize the fifth dimension as everything moving really fast and the third dimension as everything slowed down, although remember that time and space do not actually exist. Separation is an unnatural state of being in the universe that can only take place in a time/space third-dimensional illusion, because in reality, nothing occurs independently. It is only in the illusion of third-dimensional reality that there is a distinction between intention, action and consequence—and that is where karma comes in.

You are the creators of karma. Karma is a delightful creation. Well done! A group of you got together at the beginning of this third-dimensional experience and came up with the idea of karma as a useful way for humans to be able to explore their free will choices more completely. The whole idea of free will is a unique concept, and there was great interest in being able to break it down and observe it. It is important to recognize that this idea you have that karma is beyond your control is incorrect. It is not something that happens to you. Even though you set something in motion and it comes back to you, it is still your choice and still your creation. Karma is simply an opportunity to understand another aspect of the experience. Because you are creating your own reality in every moment, you must assume that in a previous lifetime, when you made the choices that are playing out karmically in this lifetime, a part of you could see the whole picture. A higher aspect of yourself was able to see both lifetimes, to see the way things were going to play out, and chose to act in the way you did so you could ultimately have the most complete experience.

I have always thought of karma and free will as a dichotomy, or in polarity with each other. I thought karma meant that you reap the consequences of your actions. So, when we are born into this life, and we reincarnate from past lives, don't we have some kind of residue that we have to work out?

That you *get* to work out, yes. As an example, imagine that in a previous lifetime you had a job you absolutely adored doing, and as a result, you became extremely wealthy and powerful. However, as a consequence of the work that you did, you manipulated and took advantage of other people. In your mind, that was an acceptable consequence of the job. Now, in this lifetime, you do not have any money, you do not have any power, and you often feel manipulated and taken advantage of. From this perspective, experiencing different aspects of a particular experience are not a third-dimensional experience possible, wanted the whole experience. You wanted to experience having power and wealth, as well as having no power and no money, simply to understand how it all fits together. Karma can be thought of as the balancing of the yin and the yang, or as the infinity symbol represented by the figure eight.

It would be useful for you to re-evaluate your current ideas about karma. Until now, karma has been a wonderful way for you to play more fully in this illusion of reality. However, if you are interested in moving beyond this illusion of reality, it is more useful to be in the present moment. When you are operating karmically, you are not present in the now, because part of the experience that you are having is tied to the past, and part of it is tied to the future. Remember that in every moment, you have everything you need to fully engage in that moment. Any time you imagine you don't and move into the illusion of lack and limitation, you are operating within a karmic cycle based on something that happened in the past or something you imagine happening in the future. If you buy into the illusion that anything you do now has to do with the past or the future, or that karma is inevitable, you are missing out on the possibility of a whole new experience.

Does karma, then, not apply to the higher dimensions, like the fifth dimension? Is it because time has sped up or that time does not exist?

If you are operating third-dimensionally, you set an intention, take action, and then there is a consequence as a result. If you are operating fifth-dimensionally, as soon as you conceive of something, you consider the whole experience. For example, if you think about cutting someone off in traffic, you will instantly see all the consequences that could play out as a result of that action. From a third-dimensional perspective, you might consider the possibility that the other driver might be angry with you, but from a fifth-dimensional perspective, you would instantly understand the fifteen thousand other outcomes that could result from that choice—and that awareness would affect your choice quite differently. This is why it is a logical next step in human evolution for you to become more telepathic and to become more in tune with other Beings, as well as with plants and animals. From that perspective, things like war, abuse and power struggles cannot exist. With complete awareness between everyone involved, they would not make any sense.

Being able to participate in such activities is one of the advantages of the third-dimensional illusion of time/space. You could spend an entire lifetime being abusive, because you are operating under the illusion that you are not aware of the consequences of your actions, whereas, if you knew what consequences your actions would have in the whole scheme of things, you could never do those kinds of things. It is not that you would feel guilty or that you would be afraid of going to prison or anything like that; it is simply that you would not make those choices if you were aware of the consequences. It is innate for you to be kind and loving. It is innate in every human being to be kind and loving, and we can include people like Hitler in that statement. If he had known what it felt like to be in his concentration camps, he could never have done what he did. In that experience, that awareness did not interest him. It did not even occur to him. Keep in mind that he was playing out a karmic cycle with all the people that he shared the holocaust experience with. Everyone who participated in that experience did so of his or her own free will.

We want you to go away from this session with a warm, fuzzy feeling for karma, because karma is not something that you try to get out of, or transcend, or earn the right to move past. It is simply a useful way for you to play with the concept of time/space. Another part of this, which we will get into in more depth in a little while, is that karma is an option and has been since 1987. When we have said this before, many people's immediate response has been, "Well, if it is an option, I don't want to do it anymore." We are not suggesting that you throw the whole idea of karma out the window; we are just suggesting that you notice when you are operating in karma, and delight in it. Notice how slowly things move right now, because very soon, that is not going to even be an option.

There are a lot of things written lately about being present in the now, but you are suggesting that nothing is static. Would you talk about how to be present in the now under these circumstances?

Yes. This is very important, because when you are operating karmically, you are not present in the now, because part of the action that you are participating in is tied into the past, and part of it is tied into the future, which again, is the beauty of it. What it means to be in the present moment is to be in possibility, not focused on manifestation. When you are in the present moment, you are not trying to make anything happen based on your past experience, and you are not making any decisions based on the future. All that is required is that you pay attention to the information that is coming to you, and make a decision based on that.

That is why it is very important for you to clear your emotional bodies. When you have an experience that reminds your emotional body of a past experience, there is an automatic response. It can be compared to when you send someone who is out of the office an email that generates an automatic response telling you that they are out of town for two weeks. As an example, if you have a conversation with someone and they are rude to you, your immediate response might be to be insulted. As soon as you become insulted, you stop fully interacting in the present situation and begin filtering the information according to when someone had been rude to you in the past. As you begin to focus on what happened before, you are instantly no longer in the present moment.

Think of how many dozens of times a day you have the opportunity to be in the present moment, and instead, you are pulled into thinking about a similar situation that has happened before. Another thing that frequently happens when someone is rude to you is that you begin to strategize about how to react, and then you contemplate how they might react to your reaction. That takes you even further away from the present moment. In that tiny amount of time, you miss all kinds of opportunities to engage in the present moment, because you are not there.

We will give you a useful analogy. Imagine that someone called to give you a million dollars, with the only caveat being that you had to return the call within thirty minutes, but you did not get home until an hour after the call was made. Because you were not home, you didn't get the message in time, and you lost the money. This is what happens to you all the time. You receive information from other people, and in the form of feelings, thoughts and ideas all the time, but if you are not in the present moment, you either miss the message or you filter it based on the past or the future and change the meaning. We don't tell you this so that you will beat yourself up about being in the past or the future. It is just to remind you that in every present moment, you have everything you need to fully engage in that moment. If you buy into the illusion that anything you do now has to do with the past or the future, you are missing the whole point of being in the now.

We want you to hear how simple this is. All you have to do is wake up in the morning, pay attention to what occurs to you to do first, and take action based on that. Then, in the middle of doing that—we don't want to say *after* doing that, because it is not always going to be that linear—something else will occur to you. So, take action based on the new thought, and carry on in this manner throughout the day. Remember, you cannot make any mistakes. You cannot make a wrong decision, because none of it is real. If you are unhappy with a choice that you make, you will have the opportunity to make another decision in the next moment or in a couple of moments down the road. You simply cannot be wrong, ever.

In counseling and psychotherapy, the big challenge is to break patterns that we are unconscious of. The first step is to bring these patterns into consciousness and realize that we cannot change anything until we are aware of the past. It is the patterns that keep us stuck to the past, but if we are conscious of being stuck in past patterns, and we are run by those patterns, how can we just change from one minute to the next?

That is a very good example, because the goal in psychotherapy and counseling is to bring you into the present to help you realize how you are acting unconsciously. That is actually not so different from what we are talking about. That is one option of how to go about doing what we are suggesting.

Because we are being run unconsciously by some very deep patterns that may even come from past lifetimes, how do we make the instantaneous switch to just making another decision?

There is a whole continuum of ways you can do this. You can go to psychotherapy and change your perspective over a period of months or years, or you can do it instantly. To do it instantly, you just have to recognize that all the patterns that you are basing your reality on are not real.

The key to this is the understanding that all of the issues that you imagine you have to work out to become enlightened or to ascend, or whatever your goal is, are simply how you are defining yourself in this present moment. Your perception of who you are is based on your past experiences, your family, your education, and what you do for work. Everything that has occurred up until this point is how you conceptualize yourself in this moment, and none of that is real.

It is important to understand that it is not a bad thing to define yourself as you do, because that is how the whole game of the illusion of third-dimensional reality works. It can be compared to the game of *Dungeons & Dragons*, a mind game where each person creates a character to play—warriors, sages and thieves, for example. It is a very complicated process. Each person comes up with a name, personal values and typical behavioral characteristics for their character. Each character must also have clearly defined weaknesses and strengths, and all of these identifying characteristics predetermine how the character will interact in any given situation.

The game is played by randomly creating scenarios, with the rolling of dice, in which the characters will interact. Essentially, it is a game during which five or six people create a shared reality in which they participate in the same experiences. It is an adventure in their minds. The part that we want to draw your attention to is that they bring the character they have created to life within the parameters of the game. Everyone knows how each character will behave in a given scenario. For example, a warrior is going to behave differently than a sage when confronted with someone who wants to fight, and a sage is going to make a different choice than a thief when gold is found, et cetera.

That is exactly what you are doing in this reality. Before you came in, you set up certain parameters. You chose a name, an energetic vibration, and a general blueprint of which twists and turns your life would take, but you were not limited to any of those prearranged choices. You merely set it up that way so you would have a variety of opportunities to make choices within the specific parameters defined by whom you believed yourself to be. Now, when we tell you that none of this is real and that you are, in actuality, just energy and light, it is not nearly as fun from your current third-dimensional perspective. However, we suggest that you consider the possibility that it actually is quite fun in a whole different way.

This brings us to another point. In *The Human Experience* session, we talked about how precious this third-dimensional experience that all of you are so anxious to end and get out of is. It is important for you to understand that it is the character that you have created for yourself to play out in this time/space that is so precious to you. You have put a great deal of energy into this creation, and you are not willing to let it go without a fight. But the thing we want you to understand is that that is not all there is to you. That is just a tiny piece of all the different characters that you could play in this vast game. You are calling this little piece of the game the whole game, and we want you to see that it is just one choice.

If you choose to throw off the illusion of who you are, it does not mean that you are going to cease to exist. In actuality, it means quite the opposite. You are going to expand to become even larger, and more possibilities are going to present themselves to you. When we talk about this time of transition, many of you think that means that you have to give something up and you may not be willing to do that. Or, you don't want to miss out on anything, and by not choosing, you keep all the options available to you. We suggest that you consider, instead, which of your many attributes you want to focus on for the next ten years. Once you choose, everything else will fall away, and you can focus on identifying yourself in that way for this next teeny, tiny ten-year period. It is only ten years! You all have had thousands and thousands and thousands of years of lifetimes; don't lose sight of the big picture here.

Isn't that fun to think about? All you have to do is choose. You get to make a choice in each moment, and all the moments together will define which character you will play next, and there are no wrong choices. You just choose something, you play it out, and then you do it all over again. Although Earth will not exist in the third dimension after 2012, keep in mind that there will be multitudes of other opportunities to experience another version of the third dimension in a time/space reality. If you move into the fifth dimension and decide that you really miss the illusion of lack and limitation, you can always choose to participate in any of those experiences.

We want you to understand that this is just one very unique moment, just as every moment in every day of your life is a unique moment. Nothing can ever be the same, because the stars will not be lined up in the same way. The person you are talking to will not be in the same exact mood, at that same exact moment, having that same exact thought. There have always been a multitude of variables present in every moment. You have simply been under the illusion that you can't assimilate all of them, so you repeatedly choose the same variables that continue to support the illusion of the character you are playing in this time/space moment. In actuality, you can assimilate and play with many different ways of being, simultaneously. We are going to give you a meditation later in this session to help you work through this.

I am a very practical person, and I look at things from a very practical point of view.

Right now, you are about eighty-five to ninety percent practical, and ten to fifteen percent other than practical. Although that ratio is very useful and has served you very well, we suggest that you consider tempering the practical a little. We suggest that you consider being maybe twenty to twenty-five percent other than practical, just for fun. If you don't like it, you can always change it back to what you have now.

That sounds like a little kid saying, "I am going to play princess now," and ten minutes later, he or she is playing a dragon or a witch or something else.

Exactly, yes. You are practical because you need to be practical in order to participate in this third-dimensional reality, so practicality is a great thing and very useful. Here is what we suggest: the next time you are trying to make a decision, notice that you have a choice to make. Then notice the choice that you make, and notice how practical it is. After you have given yourself credit for your practical choice, while keeping it as an option, also consider what might be the most impractical option. Just consider it. You can still go ahead and do the practical thing if that is want you want to do, but at the same time, allow yourself to consider what the impractical choice would be, just for the fun of it. You do not have to act on it, and it does not have to interfere with your practical life. Get into the habit of looking at both sides of everything and always considering other possibilities for everything that you do. Remember, there are never only two choices, so always contemplate a variety of options.

This is important, because there are so many variables in every moment, and you are missing all those possibilities. Until now, your goal has been to stay linear and focused on one possibility at a time so that you do not cease to exist third-dimensionally. Being linear is very useful while participating in the illusion of limitation, so do not be so anxious to throw the whole idea out the window. Instead, get used to operating from both perspectives simultaneously.

The first thing that is going to happen for many of you, once you get the hang of doing this, is that you are going to recognize that you can still maintain this third-dimensional illusion as the character that you have chosen to play. Consider the possibility that you are already experiencing a simultaneous reality in this very moment, perhaps as a dolphin in the ocean or perhaps in non-human form in another dimension. Being able to recognize yourself participating in two different experiences can be compared to manipulating two puppets at the same time, one on each hand. Don't worry that someone in this reality will notice that you are not here half of the time, because you already have not been here half of the time anyway, and no one has noticed so far!

In the creative process, imagination is the foundation element, but we seem to be on the borderline between illusion, delusion and imagination.

What makes you think that there is a borderline?

Well, I lived an illusion about somebody for twenty-five years, and I do not want to repeat that again. Where is the fine line when we straddle some sense of reality with a reality check and are not floating up in our imagination to the point where we are spacey?

There are several issues here. Ultimately, you want to give in to what you call your imagination. However, when you consider that possibility, you imagine that you will lose control of this reality. You worry that if you completely give in to that part of yourself, that the bills won't get paid, that you won't remember to keep the appointments you have made, that the laundry won't get done, that you will forget to eat...all those kinds of things. You become concerned that if you stop focusing on keeping it together, that it is all going to fall apart and you are not going to be able to sustain yourself physically anymore. To a certain degree, that is true, and that is why those concerns are there. You have programmed your mind to believe that you need to stay in physicality in order to exist in the third dimension. So, if you even consider the idea of giving in to the idea that this is all an illusion, your mind is programmed to dissuade you. From your mind's perspective, it is all or nothing. Your mind is not programmed to conceptualize how to function well third-dimensionally and to also be able to exist multidimensionally. The reason for that is because you do not become multidimensional through your mind.

When your mind gets a glimpse of what you are considering, it freaks out, because it thinks, "I cannot compute all that at once. I am in danger! Danger, Will Robinson! Something is wrong! Oh no! Stop doing that!" and then it shuts down. That is why you have those moments in a meditation or during a workshop, or even when you come to these sessions, where for just an instant, you get the whole picture and you begin to understand how it all fits together. Once your mind realizes what you are considering, it panics, and you immediately consciously forget whatever you just had a complete understanding of.

Your mind, which is in charge of keeping you third-dimensional, is just doing its job. That is why we always tell you to give your mind a break. Distract your mind while allowing other parts of your brain to explore some of these possibilities. Then, after a while, you can prove to your mind that it is possible for you to move into multidimensional awareness and to maintain your third-dimensional expression at the same time.

The five to six percent of your brain that you currently use is your mind. That is not to minimize the importance of your mind. We do not want you to think that your mind is not important as you move into fifth-dimensional awareness, because quite the opposite is true. What is unique about this transition is that your mind is an integral part of it. It is the inclusion of your mind that defines you as a hybrid human. In order to be a 3D/5D human, the inclusion of your mind is necessary. You will have to act as a mediator between your mind and the new awareness that you are moving into. Find out what all sides want, pay attention to what all sides need, and notice what you need to stay third-dimensional while striving to become multidimensional.

Many of you already do this; you already have one foot in each world. What we would like to encourage you to do is to gradually move away from the third dimension as the primary focus, while not letting it go completely. The way you currently conceptualize this is that you imagine yourself trying to understand the fifth dimension, trying to understand ascension, trying to understand all these multidimensional concepts. Every time you do, you base it all in a third-dimensional version of reality. You have been wondering how to move from the third dimension to the fifth dimension, and what you need to do to prepare your body for ascension. You actually have it backwards. What you need to do is bring your multidimensional awareness into your third-dimensional reality, and your physical body will then adjust to contain the higher vibrational energy.

You envision trying to move towards something from this experience that seems so real to you, when, in fact, what you call reality is itself the dream. This experience is a tiny piece of the whole picture, and you are trying to make this experience the whole reality and to base everything else on the illusion of third-dimensional reality. This is a time/space, third-dimensional experience, and the awareness that you are moving into cannot be contained within an illusion of limitation. To move more fully into your true expression, you will have to redefine who you are beyond the confines of the third-dimensional character that you currently identify yourself as.

How do we integrate it smoothly? I mean, you say we do not use our minds that much, and to not emphasize the mind, so what do we emphasize?

As we suggested earlier, a good place to start is to consider impractical possibilities as you make small choices in your everyday life. For example, let's say you are making cookies, and you go to the refrigerator only to find that you do not have any eggs. What would the logical solution be? You need to go to the store and buy eggs, right? Then, as you are in your car on the way to the store to buy eggs, consider what some impractical solutions might be. What would have been a completely impractical solution? Does anyone have any idea?

Use applesauce...

Not make them...

Those are still really practical.

Go buy a chicken...

Go buy a chicken. That is good, very impractical, and exactly the kind of thing we want you to consider. Are there any other suggestions?

Chuck the whole thing...

Or manifest them right there...

There you go: "or manifest them right there." Or have someone drop by and give you some cookies. Look how hard it is to think in an impractical way. You are all so good at being practical. Well done. Because you are so adept at being practical and logical, it might take you the entire way to the grocery store to come up with something impractical. So, this is the challenge that we give to you: take every opportunity you can to consider impractical possibilities when faced with a choice. We are not suggesting that you make any major life changes at this point. For example, we don't suggest that you quit your job, knowing that the practical thing to do would be to get another job, and then consider that an impractical thing would be to sit on your couch for six weeks, and choose to do that. That might not be the place to start with this exercise.

Because you make hundreds of small decisions every day, you can begin playing with this in all kinds of ways. Here is another example: when you come to a red stoplight, normally you stop so that you do not cause an accident. What would be an unpractical thing to do? Can you think of anything? What would an impractical option be?

Go home...

To manifest yourself on the other side...

Yeah, to go up, manifest up...

Yes, exactly. Look how good you are at this! Go through your day and consider impractical ways of doing things just for the fun of imagining them. Do not try to analyze them. Do not try to figure them out. Just start by imagining them, and begin to notice how many other possibilities there are in every moment, in addition to the one you choose. Begin to consider the possibility that your experience is not limited to one reality.

Imagine going through your day and considering all kinds of new possibilities for each of the mundane decisions that you make all the time. It is going to seem a bit time-consuming at first to consider ten possibilities for everything, instead of simply making a logical choice. You might wonder how you will get anything done. Maybe the point is not to get as much done. We are not saying to stop being productive, but we are saying to begin to consider that the way you are creating your reality is only one of a million possible ways to do it. We are not asking you to entirely throw out the character that you are playing. We are merely asking you to consider that being that character is only a small part of how you can express yourself in this reality. You can keep your name. You can keep your identity. You can keep your history and your future. But we suggest that you consider all of that as a starting point, and build from there.

How does grace fit in with all of this?

Grace is another aspect of the same concept that includes karma and free will. Grace is at a different place on the continuum. Karma is on one end and is long and drawn out. Grace is on the other end and is continually shifting. They fit together perfectly. Grace is one answer to the questions asked earlier about how to get into this moment, and how not to react, subconsciously or unconsciously, to everything that you are not consciously aware of. All you have to do is to understand and to accept the concept of grace, which is that everything can completely shift in a moment.

So, is grace a fifth-dimensional idea?

Yes. Grace is a fifth-dimensional technology, but it is possible to invoke grace while in the third dimension. We are going to be working with grace in the meditation that we are going to do.

When you say information that comes from the fifth dimension cannot come in through the mind because it has to come in through other ways, did I hear you say that it comes through other parts of your mind?

It comes through other parts of your brain. You know how scientists claim that most humans only use five or six percent of their brain? That five or six percent is your mind. Another way of looking at it is that fifth-dimensional information comes in through your heart, because creation is love—but we don't mean romantic love. We suggest that you imagine a little heart in your head, somewhere in your brain, and let the information come into this heart in your head, as opposed to coming into your mind. You can imagine it as a heart that changes into the flower of life. Then, see it change into a spinning merkaba. Imagine a fifth-dimensional holographic merkaba heart in your brain, and begin allowing information to come in that way sometimes, instead of always through your mind.

Does that have any relationship to the pineal gland? I have always felt that is the heart of the pineal.

Yes, exactly.

What about all those people who have their pineal glands calcified?

They have made that choice, because having a fully functioning pineal gland was getting in the way of the illusion. Because they were constantly aware of multidimensional information, they were unable to fully participate in the third-dimensional illusion of reality. It seems like such a serious thing when your pineal gland is not operating anymore, and it seems that it is going to take a lot of work to get it functioning again. But that is not true; it can be undone in a moment. When you imagine a pineal gland that appears to be calcified, you think about it third-dimensionally. If you envision looking at someone's calcified pineal gland in his or her head, it appears to be closed off with a wall around it.

That is what you would see from a third-dimensional perspective. Yet, if you could see just beyond the wall, it is working perfectly fine. What you don't realize is that the wall is holographic, and it does not really exist. The person has simply placed it there to trick him or herself. What we want you to consider is how complicated it is to do that, and to realize that people who appear to be shut down and operating solely third-dimensionally, and who appear not to have any conceptualization of all these things that we are talking about simply have a holographic wall in front of their fully-operating pineal gland. Look how fifth-dimensional they have to be to do that! So, the next time that you look at someone who seems to not get it, acknowledge how much effort it is taking for him or her to block their divinity, and appreciate that they are doing an amazing job.

Is that why there is the illusion that we have no free will, because all of this stuff is in place, and people are not aware of it?

Yes. It can be compared to the way traffic works. People know that red lights mean to stop, green lights mean to go and yellow lights mean to yield. Most people adhere to traffic laws because they understand that they exist to make driving safe. The same principle applies to the concept of karma; adherence to certain rules is necessary for the illusion of karma to play out. It was a collective consciousness agreement that set it in motion and by which everyone agreed to play until 1987. It was always an option to not participate in karma, but that would have meant missing out on a significant aspect of the third-dimensional experience, so very few Beings chose that option.

I am still struggling with the average person on the planet who is asleep. Is everyone going to awaken in the next ten years?

No, not everyone.

So is it just a matter of accepting that this is how it is, these are the choices that they made and just...

We are not talking about merely accepting their choices. We are talking about embracing their choices. Instead of worrying about them, you might think something like, "Wow, what a cool choice! That one never even occurred to me! You want to participate in war, and you want to move to another third-dimensional planet, and to explore the possibility of moving into a full-blown nuclear war. Wow!" We are not talking about acceptance; we are talking about complete enthusiasm for how well they are participating in the illusion that they are separate from each other.

What we want you to understand is that it takes a tremendous amount of energy for them to create the illusion that they are participating in. They are just deeper in the game, deeper in the dream, than you are in this moment. There was a time when you were there yourself. Try to remember what that felt like. Remember what it was like to be that unaware, what it was like to get such a kick out of density. Begin to look at how well and how uniquely others are creating their reality. So, back to the question about if everyone is going to wake up, the answer is no. There is a whole continuum of choices that are going to be made, and each one will be based on what is most interesting to that individual at that moment in time. Many people are still very interested in playing with the idea of karma. For those people, there will be a multitude of opportunities to continue doing so.

Are there any ways we can positively influence the consciousness of these people?

There is no purpose in doing that, and by attempting to do so, you assume that your illusion of reality has more validity than theirs does. Choosing density and choosing to operate under the illusion of third-dimensional reality is not better or worse than choosing to becoming enlightened and incorporating more light, or ascending. It is just different. You do not need to save anyone or to worry about anyone else. Everyone is fine. We truly want you to hear this. What you are seeing of people is only five percent of who they really are. It can be compared to an iceberg, where there is only a little tiny piece above the water, and the bulk of it is underneath. That is what you are seeing in these people. You are buying into the characters that they are playing. It may look like they are unenlightened, unhappy, addictive personalities who are leading miserable existences. You might assume that they must not have the options that you have, and therefore, don't understand how their lives could be different. You may then take it upon yourself to enlighten them; however, you need to remember that they are the same infinitely powerful Beings that you are, with all the same opportunities that you have.

But that seems to be the feeling of the Earth right now. I mean, it is not just making a judgment on individuals, saying that they do not get it or that they do not have a clue. The feeling of consciousness that incorporates our everyday life is not comfortable. It does not feel right.

If it does not feel right for you, then the reality that you are creating does not fit anymore. It is time for you to make another choice for yourself, not for you to decide that anyone else is going down the wrong path. What is important here is that the reality that you perceive to be all around you, and that seems to indicate that the world is in a sorry state right now, is merely one of many possible realities. With just a slight alteration of your perception, you can see that there is more light on the planet now than there has been since the times of Atlantis. It is simply a matter of what you choose to focus on.

We highly recommend that you cancel any magazine subscriptions that perpetuate the reality that is no longer of interest to you, such as *Newsweek* and *Time*. Stop watching the news on television or listening to it on the radio. Do not read the newspaper, and begin to focus on the realities that are of greater interest to you at this time. By participating in the perpetuation of the mass media, you are allowing your world to be defined by the mass consciousness version of reality. It is of utmost importance that you consciously choose whom you spend your time with, and consciously choose where you focus your energy. Where you choose to direct your energy is going to determine what your reality looks like. By changing what you surround yourself with, you can change everything in a moment.

Couldn't you turn the news on and watch President Bush on the TV and see the tip of his iceberg, and then look down and see the whole iceberg, and not be bothered, and be able to see that this is only a game and not real?

Yes, watching President Bush speak is a good example of the power of the mass consciousness version of reality. Imagine that all the people in the United States are tethered into him, and imagine that he can pick up on all that energy and really quickly synthesize it. Then, he says what the majority of them want to hear. Think about him like this really cool, metaphysical computer, because that is, in essence, what he is. He is not in charge of creating this reality; he has offered to play a role that many Beings wanted someone to play out.

That is another approach to take, although we suggest that if you have been really immersed in the media version of reality, you completely step out of it for a while, because your participation has established habitual reactions to what you perceive as the reality around you. It is one option to experience a reality that is created by decisions made on a mass consciousness level. Instead of consciously experiencing every moment and becoming aware of all the multiple possibilities in every moment, the other end of the continuum is to not take any personal responsibility, and to make decisions on a collective level. That is what many Beings have decided to do in many countries around the world, including the United States. But keep in mind that it is simply one of many possible experiences.

Instead of experiencing a reality created by taking personal responsibility, Beings participating in that version of reality buy into the illusion that they have no personal power and allow reality to be determined for them on a mass consciousness level. That version of reality is not better or worse than a reality in which more personal responsibility is taken; it is just different. When you step out of the mass consciousness version of reality for a while, you will begin to get more of a sense of who you are outside of the collective. Once you have done that, you can then go back into the collective experience in whatever limited ways you want, and it will look different to you. We just want you to recognize how it all fits together and how everyone, regardless of what it looks like, has agreed to play his or her part.

A good example of this is to consider everything that has happened since September 11. There has been a continuum of responses, from peace prayers to war, both individually and collectively, to the deaths of so many "innocent people." We love that term, "innocent people." It was the mass consciousness understanding that those Beings who died had no choice and that their lives were unfairly and violently taken from them. When you participate in that version of the experience, all your victim issues from every lifetime you have ever had come into play, and you begin to allow the mass consciousness choices to create your experience.

To continue with our example, at one point early in the war, American soldiers inadvertently killed a group of women and children. According to the mass consciousness version of reality, it is okay for the military to kill the bad guys, but it is not okay to kill women and children. It is actually the same thing. When the pieces don't seem to fit so neatly together anymore, you are seeing a crack in the mass consciousness version of reality, and that is a good place to start prying it open. Begin to notice when pieces of the apparent reality do not seem to fit, think about why they do not fit, and consider other possibilities to explain what appears to be happening. Remember that, without exception, everyone who participates in any given experience has agreed to play his or her part.

Consider the possibility that each one of the so-called "innocent victims" who was killed in the September 11th bombings chose that experience. Remember that energy can never be destroyed; it simply changes form. And remember, too, that because this is a free will experience, no one can change form against his or her will. There are no mistakes. No individual or group or government has the power to destroy another person, another race, or another country. It simply cannot happen in a free will experience.

It seems like when you get down to it, your perception is your reality, and that is all it is.

That is the bottom line, yes. Remember that this is supposed to be fun. It is just a game. As you alter your perception, you change your reality. You can change it on a whim, and then, if you want to, you can change it back. Look how much energy that frees up when you do not have to worry about making the wrong choice.

What is your definition of reality?

There is no reality. Nothing is real. Reality is an illusionary construct that appears to be real.

Well, you are sitting right now on that couch.

Not really.

I mean, sometimes we can get into these mind games, but you can also play with words and meanings and definitions and terms and it gets into this... it is like this void, this vortex where nothing is anything.

Yes, that is it, the void vortex where nothing is anything. That is it; you just named it, and in the void vortex, there is nothing to do. Now, we know that your next question is going to be, "If there is nothing to do, what do I do?" And the answer is, "Do whatever occurs to you to do."

Whatever occurs to you in the moment?

Yes. Doing whatever feels good is a good place to start, although it is still third-dimensional, because there is an inherent judgment there. It is still a good place to start, because so many things that you do, you do out of obligation, not because they feel good to you. Here is another good first step to take: when you cannot quite do what feels good in every moment, at least consider what you could do instead. Go ahead and do what you have to do, or not, but consider other options.

In the morning, as you are getting ready to go to work, ask yourself, "If I was not going to go to work today, what would I do instead?" You might even find on many days that your answer will be, "If I could do anything that I wanted to do today, I would choose to go to work." It is important to recognize that the actions that you take are your choice, because it is this acknowledgement that you are operating within free will that will help you remember that it is all you. Nothing that happens to you is inevitable. Even if you have set a karmic pattern into motion that you are currently playing out, you can change your mind at any time and there is no penalty. What is it in Monopoly? You do not pass go and you do not collect two hundred dollars when you go to jail. That does not happen. There is no penalty for anything, ever.

If you cannot quite get to the point of doing what you want to in every moment, at least consider what you would like to be doing in every moment. Then, if you choose to do what you feel obligated to do, do not beat yourself up about it. Just consider what else you could do, and notice that you are making a choice. That is another thing. It is really important to make choices. Stop sitting on the fence. Do not be afraid to choose. Do not be afraid to recognize that you may not be behaving in an enlightened manner at all times. Perhaps you still think badly about the person driving in front of you, because he or she is driving like an idiot. You might find yourself thinking, "That person is a jerk." And then your next thought might be, "That was such an unenlightened thing to think. I probably just set a whole karmic cycle in motion." Pay attention to the realities that you are creating with your thoughts. Remember, there are no penalties for anything, ever.

You keep using the words "change" and "to choose." You can choose in a very conscious way, but you can also choose in an unconscious way.

Exactly, and we are talking about the conscious way.

So, how do you make that shift from the unconscious choosing? Let's say you had a relationship that did not work out, and you do not want to repeat that same pattern. How do you step out of that pattern and never have to repeat it?

The pattern does not exist in this present moment. That was in the past. A pattern indicates a past, present and future perspective; in other words, a third-dimensional perspective of reality. Let's say that you meet an interesting person and begin a new relationship.

In this new relationship, perhaps there is a situation when you find yourself in a familiar scenario, and because you remember being in this place before, you take action based on your experience in past relationships. This brings the past pattern into your current relationship.

For example, perhaps in a past relationship, someone said that he or she was going to call you, and then didn't, and that turned out to be a pattern for the relationship. Throughout the relationship, this person rarely followed through on anything that he or she promised, and it made you crazy. So, in this new relationship, when the person says he or she is going to call, and then they don't, you have the opportunity in that moment to choose what that means. Now, you have to understand that the choice you make about what this means has nothing to do with why the person is not calling, and it has nothing to do with why the person in the other relationship did not follow through on anything. It simply has to do with what it means to you in the present moment.

Choosing to repeat the pattern is one of the options in the present moment. You may choose to be angry with that person for not calling, and that would be a perfectly valid response based on your past experience. But also consider the other options that you could choose. For example, maybe he or she lost your phone number and is devastated, because he or she really likes you. Keep in mind that choosing to repeat the pattern is only one of endless possibilities of how your current reality can play out. If you choose to behave as if you are still operating in the pattern, just notice that you are making that choice, instead of choosing to feel as if the pattern is inevitable.

But it feels the same...

But it is not, because no two moments can ever be the same. When you make choices, you need to begin to differentiate between what those choices are based on. Are they based on the past? Are they based on the future? Can you recognize that this is a place that you have never been before? In every moment, look at more than one option. Consider at least three or four. Even though you may cognitively understand that it is possible to operate outside of karmic patterns, you just do not remember how. You need to practice, and the place to begin is to notice what you are basing your choices on in each moment. Just observe yourself making choices for a while, and consider multiple options each time you are presented with a choice. Do not be upset if you find that you are still operating in patterns based upon the past or on how you perceive the future. Remember, too, that it is always an option to change your reality through grace; however, if you are not ready to do that in this moment, that is perfectly fine, as well.

What does it mean to change your reality through grace?

Changing your reality through grace means to immediately operate outside of karma. We are going to give you an opportunity to practice making choices in the meditation. Keep in mind that each time you are offered a choice, it is not your one and only chance to choose. We are going to ask you to instantaneously choose, and we suggest that you do not filter the choices through your past experience, or based on the future, by analyzing all the possible outcomes. Just choose in that moment. You can go back and do this meditation at any time and re-choose as many times as you want to. This is an opportunity for you to practice being in the present moment and to decide whether you want to invoke karma or grace. Okay, let's do the meditation.

☸

We want you to begin by picturing yourself holding one of those Easter eggs with a large opening on one end where you can look inside and see the little scenes. As you imagine that you are holding this Easter egg in your hand, closely observe its details. Notice what it looks like on the outside, notice what color it is, and notice how big it is. Does it just sit in the middle of the palm of your hand, or does it extend from your wrist to your fingertips? How wide is it? Is it only one color? What kind of design is on it? Are there little squiggles? Are there flowers? What does it taste like? Hold it up to your tongue and taste it. It is clean. It is your egg, and no one else has touched it. Hold your hand up and look at it from the bottom. What does it look like from that angle? Now, look inside your egg and focus on the scene. What do you see? Are there people in there? Are there animals? Is there an ocean? Mountains? A forest?

All of a sudden, you find that you are not looking in the egg anymore, but you are inside the egg. Everything that was small is suddenly all around you. What do you see? Turn all around. Look in all directions. Think to yourself, "I cannot believe all of this was inside that little tiny egg. It is so vast. There are so many different possibilities in here." Now, look down at where you are standing. Notice that you are standing in a circular area, and there are multiple paths going out from where you are standing. Go stand in front of one of those paths. Stay in the circle, in the middle, but stand at the beginning of one of those paths. As you stand there, notice that you feel the potential of what might happen if you go down that path. As soon as you feel that, decide if that path is interesting to you or not. You are still in the center of the circle at this point; do not go down the path yet.

Now, go stand in front of another path, and do the same thing. As you stand there, you can feel the possibility and potential of what might happen if you go down that path. Ask yourself if you have ever felt this before. Does this path seem familiar, or does it feel different? You are still in the center of the circle; do not go down that path, either. Now, take a few minutes to go stand in front of one, two, three, or however many other paths you want to. Stay in the center of the circle, and just feel what experiences the different paths have to offer. Feel the potential and the possibility of what might happen if you choose each unique path. Remember to ascertain if each path feels familiar or if it offers something new...

Now, it is time to choose. You can go down a path that you have not stood in front of yet, or you can go back to any of the paths you have just visited and choose one. Do not hesitate, just choose. You can always come back to the circle and re-choose. Choose a path and stand at the beginning of it. Notice again whether it feels familiar or new. Do not judge it. Do not question it. Now, slowly move out of the circle and begin following the path you have chosen. Take a moment now to see where this path takes you....

After a while, notice that there is someone or something on the path ahead of you. When you reach them, you realize that they have a gift for you. Choose whether or not to accept the gift...

Walk for a little longer. Notice again that there is someone or something on the path ahead of you. When you reach them, you realize that you can ask them a question. Ask your question and listen for the answer...

Notice that it occurs to you that this is just one of the many paths that you could have chosen. As soon as you remember the circle from which all of the paths extended in different directions, each offering different potential and possibility, you instantly find yourself back in the circle again. Smile to yourself in anticipation of which path you are going to follow next. As soon as you have that thought, you find yourself immediately outside of the experience, holding the egg in your hand, looking at it from outside. Remember what color the egg is. Remember how big it is. Remember the designs on it. Remember what it tastes like. Know that you can go into this egg and go into the circle and follow any path any time you want to. When you are ready, slowly come back to this room and open your eyes.

We suggest that when you find yourself deep within the illusion of third-dimensional reality and are having a hard time making a decision, or just having a hard time being in your life, you see yourself in this circle of choices and consider all the different options. Let your mind play between the meditation and what appears to be your reality. Gently remind yourself that this is but one of a multitude of options present in every moment. Know that you are operating at many points simultaneously on a continuum. You are creating from the illusion of karma and you are creating within grace, and know that the two of them are intermingled in every moment.

☸

Consider that in one moment, you can instantaneously transform your reality through grace; the next moment is long and drawn out in a beautiful karmic experience, and then you move into grace again. It can be compared to Morse code--a long line and a dot, a long line and a dot. Imagine karma as a line and grace as a dot. Begin to notice when you are enjoying a karmic experience and when you are exploding into a graceful moment. Know that each is unique, and do not judge them. Simply notice which one is defining your present moment, or which one you just came out of, or which one you are planning to move into next. Notice how much you operate in this past-present-future concept. Know that virtually all of your third-dimensional consciousness is based within the concept of time/space, and consider what it might be like if your reality was not defined by the concept of time/space.

Earlier, you said that we could instantaneously change our reality, and lately, I have this feeling in my head—it feels like something flips and it actually feels like, for a second, something turns over in my head...

Yes, it does, and if you haven't noticed it before, you will notice it now. It is as if when you flip like that, there is a whole new surface of possibility. That is such a third-dimensional way of explaining it. Each flip opens up all kinds of possibilities, and if you were to flip again, you would not flip back to the side that you just flipped from. It is unique each time. Each flip presents you with a whole new set of possibilities. That is what we meant when we said that no two moments could ever be the same. Although it may appear that you are just flipping from one side to another, in reality, each time you flip, an entirely new set of opportunities is presented. It is important that you recognize that it is new, and that you not filter it through your past experience.

Don't think about it too much. Just enjoy the flips. Keep in mind that, more often than not, you don't notice when you flip. A more common experience is that you suddenly have all these new ideas and thoughts and possibilities that had not occurred to you before. Usually, as soon as you flip, you do not bother spending time thinking about the flip, and you just move into the new experience, because you have all this new energy to work with. You do not spend time analyzing what just happened or thinking about what your reality was like before all of these new possibilities presented themselves. It is irrelevant, because you are now immersed in a whole new experience.

This happens to you all the time. You may feel like you are still carrying around so much of your old baggage, but you really aren't.

The reason you do not know that you are different is because as soon as you make these flips, what came before is completely gone, so you no longer have a point of reference to notice what has changed. Essentially, you are continuously making quantum leaps in consciousness, and as soon as you make a leap, you have no interest in what happened before the leap. This makes it difficult for you to gauge how much progress you are making.

Trust us—you are making exponential progress! You have moved so much more into the present than you were before this session, or than you were last week, or even than you were six months ago. You are more consciously in the present than you could even have conceived of a year ago. You do not have to learn how to be in the present. All you have to do is set the intention—"I want to be in the present moment"—and then don't give it another thought.

Why is 1987 significant when we are talking about karma?

The harmonic convergence took place in 1987, and at that time, Earth stopped holding karma for humanity. It can be compared to the hard drive of a computer in the sense that when you turn it off, the hard drive will retain the information that you put onto it, and when you turn the computer back on, you can pick up where you left off. Up until 1987, Earth held karma for humanity. At the time of the harmonic convergence, all Beings had the option to move into grace or to hold their karma in their own energy field. Holding karma in your energy field keeps you in density. Earth chose not to do it anymore after 1987, because she is very clearly on the ascension path and wanted to lighten her energetic field. Once you make the choice to operate outside of karma, your energy field inevitably begins to speed up and incorporate more light. The harmonic convergence heralded the possibility of ascension for humanity en masse.

I was on the website of a group that I was associated with, and they made a statement that they do not take credit cards as payment for classes, because it is buying into and feeding into the system of karma because of the way the credit card companies charge high rates of interest. What is your take on that?

The exchange of financial energy in any form is karmically based. Money is not real. Engaging with money in the form of credit cards, in the form of gold, in the form of cash, in all forms, is karmic. Financial energy is assigned a specific value and is exchanged for something else of equal assigned value. When you participate in a financial energy exchange, you take one form of energy in the present and simply change it into another form of energy in the future. The concept of money is entirely based in karma.

How could they offer classes and not participate in karma?

The classes themselves are karmic. Any time someone offers a service that is perceived as information that someone else needs, that is immediately karmic. The assumption that someone does not have something in this moment that they are going to have in the future is karmic. That group is in the process of beginning to dismantle the concept of karma, and that is where they chose to start. Their logic is not entirely sound at this point, but they are beginning to break it down, and that is as good of a place to start as any.

But it sounds to me like they are making a judgment against credit cards, that one kind of money is better than another kind of money.

The fact that they can define financial energy in different terms is something that can only be done from a third-dimensional perspective, but keep in mind that for them to even consider making a differentiation means that they are beginning to understand that it is not real at any level. And that is ultimately where they are going to end up.

Money is karmic, because there is a perceived need or a desire, and it is believed that an exchange of financial energy will meet that need or desire. Karma is in play any time there is a past, present and future involved. With money, if there is a perceived lack that is resolved with the exchange of financial energy, then it is karmic. If you are going to operate with money at all, it is going to be karmic. To get out of operating with financial energy in a karmic sense, you have to recognize that you do not need anything. Consider the possibility that you have absolutely everything that you need in this moment, and that you can trust that the same will be true in the next moment and the next.

Is that a third-dimensional or a fifth-dimensional concept?

You supercede third-dimensional reality as soon as you recognize the karmic nature of money. You cannot have that awareness and still operate solely from a third-dimensional perspective. Remember that it is possible to be aware of yourself third-dimensionally and multidimensionally at the same time. Understanding that karma is a choice is a good way to begin to recognize that you cannot completely define yourself in terms of your physical expression.

As you delve more deeply into the experience of the present moment, you are going to be able to perceive multiple expressions of yourself simultaneously. For many of you, the first step in this direction will be the ability to perceive yourself as your third-dimensional character and as participating in another version of reality at the same time. Many of you are already playing with this in your dreams, and we invite you to begin to become more fully aware of all that you are in every waking moment, as well. Remember that karma is merely one of a multitude of experiences available to you.

Love and Emotion

"It is only when love exists that creation can occur."

Can you talk about what we consider love versus what the Records are calling love?

Love, as most human beings understand it, could be interchanged with need. If you consider the popular culture perspective of love, as portrayed in movies and music for example, true love is demonstrated by saying, "I need you," or "You complete me." These statements imply that the individuals do not consider themselves complete without the presence of the other person in their lives. In other words, they define themselves in terms of the relationship. It is only from a third-dimensional point of view that it is possible to imagine yourselves to be separate from anyone else and that another person might have a missing piece of your happiness. It is really a very absurd idea.

Love is literally the energy that fuels creation. It is only when love exists that creation can occur. We are going to discuss this from several different perspectives throughout this talk, because love is an abstract concept and, as such, difficult to conceptualize. In reality, love is not something that you can talk about; it is not something you can define; it is not something you can point at and say you have it or do not have it. As a result, there are some inherent difficulties in talking about love, but we are going to do it anyway because it is of utmost importance that you truly understand the energy of love in order to move into conscious creation of your reality.

All of you have experienced love. You can never be without love. Many of you believe that there are times when you have love in your lives and times when you are without love. That cannot be. You cannot be without love. Love is not external; it is something that you carry within you. When you feel as if there is not love in your life, it is simply that you are not recognizing the love that you are. Love is a feeling, but it is not an emotion. The most useful way to think about love is in terms of an unending, continuously available flow of energy. Love is within you and around you always. You exist in a universe that is comprised of the energy of love.

How do love and emotion interact?

Emotion can be used to gauge how consciously you are interacting with the love that you are and with the love that is available to you. Emotion is an indicator of the degree of love that you have been using to create your reality. Every time you become aware of an emotion, it is an opportunity to reevaluate what you are creating in this time/space moment and to make another choice. If you were to be fully conscious of emotion, you would experience it as a continual flow of information. At this time, you do not recognize emotion on that level, because you judge your emotions and believe that some emotions are more acceptable than others. Consequently, you disregard and deny those emotions that you consider to be unacceptable. Once you become more aware of how you experience emotion, you will be able to use your emotional information to monitor the degree of love present in your creation of reality.

I think of the words 'love' and 'passion' as interchangeable. Do the Records equate passion with love?

When you are truly aware of love, you do not experience it as an emotion. Love is an energy. There is no separation between you and love. Passion is an emotion. Passion is experienced as an expression of enthusiasm toward a particular person or idea. Conceptualize a continuum between love and fear, with fear being the furthest you can go away from love. Fear is not the complete absence of love; it is, instead, the furthest you can go into the illusion that you are operating away from love. On this continuum, there are multitudes of emotions, some which you are currently aware of and many of which you are not. When you engage with the emotions toward the fear end of the continuum, your choices and actions tend to be reactive, and are more proactive when you engage with the emotions toward the love end.

Engaging out of fear causes you to move away from something, and engaging out of love allows you to move toward something. You can ascertain where you are on the continuum by determining whether you are moving toward your goals and dreams or away from unhappiness and discomfort. Once you get a handle on this, you are going to recognize that you are not at any one place on the continuum at any given moment. Understanding the true nature of love will help you become more consciously aware that you experience multiple versions of reality at the same time, and that each version of reality originates from a different point on the continuum.

Is there any distinction between intensity and passion? In other words, does the degree of intensity that you have about a possibility relate to how likely it is that it will manifest?

Passion is an emotion and intensity is not. You are using the word intensity to mean the degree of intent, when in fact, the degree of intensity is irrelevant. A thought that momentarily passes through your mind is as powerful as a desire that you become obsessed about. You can simply allow a thought that occurs to you to move into manifestation, or you can have a thought occur to you and choose to visualize the outcome, plan out the details and reinforce it with continual affirmations. Both techniques have the same power; it is simply a matter of how much control your mind thinks you have over the process.

Does that mean that your passing thoughts set events into motion?

Yes. And think about what that means. Think about what you could be setting into motion thousands of times each day. This is the perfect direction to go next, because when you have an idea or intent, regardless of how much intensity you put into it, it sets something into motion. And once it is set into motion and is manifested into reality and other people begin to engage with what you have created, you receive feedback from your manifestation of reality in the form of emotion. And it is through this emotional information that you have multiple opportunities to change what you have set into motion. Regardless of whether you are awake or asleep, there is a continual stream of emotional information coming to you. It is an incredibly rapid feedback loop. What you have done is to identify the most problematic emotions and the most enjoyable emotions, and worked out logical mental ways to deal with them, so that you can function within your reality without consciously engaging with the full spectrum of emotional energy available to you. Beings who are not able to make cognitive sense of emotional information suffer from what you term 'mental illness,' because they do not seem to be able to effectively participate in this feedback loop.

Most Beings who are able to function well third-dimensionally have shut off much of the information that is coming into them and only consciously choose to acknowledge part of the reality they are creating. If you think about this from a psychological perspective, reality can be experienced consciously, subconsciously or unconsciously, as well as on a mass consciousness/archetypical level. Each of these perspectives is useful in slowing this incredibly fast feedback loop to a degree that it can be broken down and analyzed so that you can understand it. In reality, however, there can be no separation.

You are all wired to fully and consciously engage with this feedback loop. This is what is meant when you hear that you use only six percent of your brain. You need to consciously engage with the constant flow of emotional information coming to you to be able to utilize the other ninety-four percent that is not currently being used. It has to do with being able to assimilate information coming in quickly, and consciously knowing what you are manifesting, receiving feedback in the form of emotional information, and making another choice. Notice that we say *making a choice*, not *taking an action*. It is making a choice. You constantly manifest reality, receive feedback, and make another choice. There is nothing more to it. There is nothing to figure out. There is nothing to analyze. It is simply a series of choices that determines the reality that you are creating at any given moment.

This is why we have been encouraging you to get in touch with what it is that you truly want to do in each moment of each day. All you have to do is get up in the morning, make a choice about what to do first, and then, based on your emotional feedback loop, choose again, and move through your day in this manner. It is imperative that you learn to trust yourself so that you can effortlessly make the choices that will create the reality you would like to manifest. When you are engaging with your reality in this manner, if you do not like a choice that you have made, it loops back to you very quickly and you get to make another choice. Know that it is not possible to make a wrong or incorrect choice. You cannot make a mistake. It is only when you do not recognize that you have all of these opportunities to make choices, and that you do not consciously choose what to manifest, that it feels like your reality is out of your control. When you slow the process down and question it, you move out of the process and do not accurately interpret the emotional information that you are receiving.

It is useful to imagine the emotional information feedback loop as a conveyor belt of emotions, and when you choose to focus on one particular emotion, fifteen others go by unnoticed. We are breaking it down and making it very mechanical to help you understand this with your mind, because in reality, the emotional information feedback loop is not that linear. The information actually comes to you in many different forms. It can come to you as a color, as a degree of light, as a sound, as a geometrical shape, as a physical sensation or as a smell. Emotional information can also take a form beyond your currently recognized senses--senses that you do not yet have an understanding of.

How does worry and focusing on old emotions affect the physical body?

Worrying slows everything down and causes the physical body to age. In reality, you do not have to age. It is possible to maintain a physical form indefinitely if you do not participate in the third-dimensional illusion. The belief that you can age, however, is a delightful concept.

Can we talk about this in terms of energy? Would you say that the love vibration is a higher, finer vibration than we currently resonate at? For example, is being depressed the opposite of being in a heightened love state?

Think about it in terms of the continuum. At the love end of the continuum, you are vibrating at a high speed. Time seems to pass quickly. You have abundant energy, and you age slowly or not at all. At the fear end of the continuum, you vibrate at a slower rate. Time seems to move more slowly. You have less energy, are more tired, and may feel lethargic or depressed and, as a result, you age more rapidly.

The whole idea of ascension is to speed up your energy so that you can move out of the third dimension and into higher dimensional awareness. As you move through the ascension process, you incorporate more light into your energy field and increase your vibration. Conscious ascension is simply becoming aware of the constant presence of love within you and around you.

Third-dimensional illusion can only exist when there is an absence of integration of the information from the emotional information feedback loop into conscious creation of reality. For example, war is a third-dimensional concept. War would never be conceived of fifth-dimensionally, because when you are fully aware of love and are conscious of the consequences of each of your choices, you would not choose to perpetrate war. The reason war is possible in a third-dimensional illusionary reality is because the feedback comes back so slowly that there is not a conceptualization in the minds of those Beings perpetrating the war of all the consequences being set into motion. This is where karma fits in. For example, it wasn't until many years after the Vietnam War that people realized the mental, emotional and physical affects upon the Vietnam veterans. Now that is an extremely slow feedback loop.

In some religions, they use the word 'ecstasy'. Can you talk about that?

Ecstasy is an emotional expression of being in the energy of love. When you are experiencing ecstasy, you have a tremendous amount of energy and love emanating through you.

Is the purpose of tantric sex to join the physical and spiritual vibrations of love?

During the act of tantric sex, the illusion of two separate individuals disappears, and their energies fuse into one expression or experience. The illusion of separation no longer exists in the ecstasy of the moment during tantric sex. If you could actually watch a couple engage in tantric sex from an energetic perspective, you would see that the Beings would not be separate during the moment of experiencing ecstasy. In that moment, they are not experiencing themselves as individuals.

If emotion is information, how do we translate how we experience the emotion into useful information?

When you become aware of emotion, allow yourself to feel it. Do not immediately make any decisions or take any action based on the emotion. Simply experience it. You will notice that once you acknowledge the emotion, it will move out relatively quickly. The only time that emotions stay for a long time is when you do not allow yourself to feel them. They will remain in your consciousness as long as possible and, eventually, as you continue to disregard them, they move into your unconscious--but they will not entirely go away until you receive the information that they have for you.

Think about when a young child falls off his or her bike and skins a knee. He or she may cry for a few minutes, but then get back on the bike and ride away like nothing ever happened, and the knee will heal perfectly within a few days. As you get older, you are not encouraged to express raw emotion in that way. When you are hurt, either physically or emotionally, you are taught to develop "a stiff upper lip," to "toughen up," to not be a "crybaby," to just "suck it up," and other such coping mechanisms. As you learn to suppress your emotions, you begin to express inappropriate anger or to withdraw into yourself when you are hurt. As a result, your body does not heal as quickly or as well as it did when you were younger. Even though your instinct is to express emotion immediately, it is socialized out of you so that you are better able to participate in the third-dimensional illusion of reality.

Consider how much information you have suppressed over time, and imagine how much energy it takes to ignore all of those messages. It can be compared to a garage that needs to be cleaned out. You know in the back of your mind that it needs to be done, but continue to contribute to the clutter, and every time you add something new, you realize that you are getting further behind. But you convince yourself that you do not have the time to deal with it right now, and the disorder becomes worse. That is what you have done with years of emotions. Every time something happens that reminds you of one of those unexpressed emotions in your garage, you add other unexpressed emotions to it, like guilt and frustration, which only serves to make the situation more overwhelming.

As a case in point, those who you call Indigo children are not very good at suppressing their emotions. As an extreme example, if someone is picking on them at school, they might just take a gun and shoot that person. They are wired differently than you are because they are not here to perpetuate a third-dimensional illusion of reality, so it is not necessary for them to learn how to suppress their emotions. They already create their versions of reality by consciously engaging with their emotional information feedback loops. For parents who have not dealt with their emotions for years, these children are quite difficult to raise, because they refuse to suppress their emotions and react quite strongly if forced to do so.

Isn't there a difference between suppression and restraint of feelings? For example, let's say a married man is attracted to his secretary. He can acknowledge his feelings of attraction, but have restraint and not act on them.

You are using the word 'restraint' as we are using the word 'choice.' In terms of your example of a married man who is attracted to his secretary, once he acknowledges his attraction, he is presented with a multitude of choices that he can make, and each choice will provide feedback for him and offer him an opportunity to choose again. Each time that he makes a choice, it presents a different situation with different circumstances. If he chooses to act on his attraction, he will experience different emotions than if he chooses not to act on it. It is the choices that he makes in response to the emotional information that will determine what will happen next in his life, not the emotions themselves.

It sounds like it is the judgment of the emotions that is the problem.

As we have said repeatedly in these sessions, simply allow yourself to feel your emotions and to suspend all judgment about them. It is okay to feel anger at the driver who has just cut you off on the road. It is possible to be angry one moment and then to be happily singing along with the radio in the next moment. Or you can choose to act on your anger, flip the other driver off and then choose to feel guilty about feeling angry and berate yourself for not behaving in an enlightened manner. Each choice presents an entirely different experience. What you experience as emotion is merely information about what you set into motion with a previous choice.

My pattern, up until this point, has been to think of 'choice' by associating it with 'action,' as in choosing whether or not to do something. I don't know how to 'choose' without 'doing,' because it feels the same to me.

Begin to focus on what feels right or what does not feel right in any given moment, and make your choices based on that. In order for this to effectively change your pattern, you must also stop questioning each choice that you make. Allow yourself to make a choice, pay attention to the emotional feedback that comes to you, and choose again. What you are doing now is making a choice, and then doubting or analyzing your decision based on the consequences that you imagine might result. When you do this, you create a loop around a single emotion, and there is no forward momentum. In order to use the emotional information feedback loop most effectively, you must focus on making choices, not on the consequences of your actions. Your actions inevitably result from your choices, and by focusing on the actions instead of the emotions, you are focusing on the end result, instead of the means that get you that result.

Becoming aware of the constant stream of emotional information available to you is an important aspect of the ascension process and is a quantum leap in taking responsibility for the conscious creation of your reality. As we encourage you to pay more attention to your emotions, we don't mean to focus on naming what you are feeling, because as soon as you name an emotion, you begin judging or analyzing it. This applies even to those emotions that you consider to be positive, as that is still a judgment.

The way you currently experience emotion can be compared to damming up a river. When you do not allow the emotional information to flow through you, and you judge or analyze it, you begin looping around a single emotion, and there is no forward momentum. This makes it difficult to stay in the present moment, because you are stuck looping in a past moment and disregarding the continual flow of emotional information that relates to the present moment.

As you spend more time engaging in the present moment, you will become increasingly adept at interpreting emotional information, and will begin to trust yourself without reservation. You will no longer focus on your actions, and you will be able to assimilate all of the emotional information being sent to you through your feedback loop. You imagine that the road before you will be as arduous as the road behind you, but we want you to know that, in fact, the road completely disappears and, instead, you will soon be flying.

If you are not in the present moment, you might not even notice that you are flying, and may feel as if you are trodding along on the same difficult path, having to learn another lesson in order to earn your divine mastery. Consider the possibility that, in this moment, you are a divine master. Begin to trust your choices without reservation. Begin to fully engage with your emotional feedback loop. Choose to move in the direction of love on the continuum and watch your manifestation of reality change all around you.

Eventually, you are going to stop moving away from the belief that you are not fully unenlightened and begin moving toward the awareness that you cannot be anything other than light and love. And that point, a spontaneous quantum shift will occur within you, and you will no longer define where you are at any given moment in terms of where you were previously. And at that point, your experience becomes less about moving toward love than about moving within love.

You need to understand that this moment is like no other moment ever before in the time/space continuum experience of earth, and know that magic can happen before your very eyes. Think about the fairytales that you knew as a child, when magic happened all of the time. Although you came to realize that magic did not seem to be part of everyday reality, you still wanted more than anything to believe that magic was possible. Find that belief again, and know that magic can happen within you. Each of you is magic. Notice we did not say that each of you can *do* magic; we said you *are* magic.

If that concept is so important, why have we lost it as we have grown older?

Because the goal, up until now, has been to forget this concept in order to experience the illusion of being limited to human form. The concept of being magic is instinctual and natural for you. What is unnatural for you is to imagine yourself as human. You have had to put a great deal of effort into pretending that you are not magic, and because you have been doing such a good job of denying your divinity over many lifetimes, it has begun to feel as if it were true. Think about how it feels when you are moving really fast in one direction, and then decide to change directions. It usually takes a few seconds to slow your momentum enough to change directions, and for a few seconds, you may continue to move in the original direction. That is a perfect analogy for your transition from perceiving yourself in limited human form to remembering your inherent divinity. Your belief that this illusionary world is real has gained a significant amount of momentum. It is this momentum and your habitual belief systems that continue to pull you away from remembering that you are magic.

Keep in mind that this imagined world of limitation has been fun for you, and the original plan was that this experience was going to continue for another few lifetimes. However, you have now decided that this is the lifetime where it comes to an end. Those of you who are still operating within karmic cycles up to this point had been anticipating the opportunity to continue to play them out into the future, and are having difficulty with the idea that you can complete everything now. Your response has been along the lines of, "Oh, I can be done now? Well, do I want to be done? I am kind of on a roll here. I am in the middle of this great karmic drama with all the roles filled and all the pieces in place. Do I really want to just stop here?"

As with any project in which you have invested a great deal of effort, it might take you a little while to let go of your old goals and ideas when you are presented with a surprising new opportunity. This is the choice that is before humanity now, and there are those who think that this is too much fun to stop now and want to play in this illusionary reality for another few thousand years. Ultimately, all beings will regain awareness of the divinity that exists within them, so it does not matter if they choose to remember now or later.

Can this be compared to driving down one street and realizing that I actually need to be on another street in order to get where I am going?

That is a great way to think about making choices. You are driving down one street when you see a sign for another street, which gives you the opportunity to choose to continue on the street that you are on or to turn onto a different one. In most cases, there is more than one way to get to a specific destination, so if you don't turn onto the street that you have just come to, you can turn onto another one farther along. This is a useful analogy for emotions, as well. The street sign is the emotion or the information, which gives you an opportunity to make a choice. To take this example a bit further, if you turn onto a street that you don't want to be on, you are presented at the next intersection with the possibility of choosing a different street. In other words, one way to conceptualize your life experience is by comparing it to driving along a freeway at great speed, continually being presented with opportunities to experience multitudes of different versions of your current reality. There are other drivers on this freeway who are also making their own choices. Some might even make the same choices that you do, and when you both get off on the same exit, you might both choose to go into the same gas station and have a conversation...or not.

The point is that you can choose to stay in a particular version of reality over several lifetimes and play it out karmically from many perspectives. It is also an option to choose to do something completely different at any time. It can be compared to making the choice to turn left at a familiar intersection and then finding yourself in an entirely different city or even a different country. We want you to be open to your reality completely shifting, like in the movie *The Wizard of Oz*, when Dorothy says, "Toto, we are not in Kansas anymore." Keep in mind that such experiences do not need to be frightening, unless, of course, you *choose* to experience fear. This transition can be as exciting, interesting and fun as you decide you want it to be.

When you talk about feeling our emotions, are you saying to equate our feelings with our bodily sensations, like goose bumps or a gut feeling? Is that how the information in the emotion is translated into feeling for us?

For some people, emotional information is experienced physically. Each individual experiences emotional information differently. Some people are very aware of physical sensations within their bodies; for others, it is as if the air around them changes. Some people feel energy around them and other people hear or see the information. Begin to notice how you receive emotional information, and keep in mind that you may not receive it in the same way all of the time. As you begin to notice how you receive emotional information it would initally be useful to do so when it appears that there is not really anything happening. Of course, there is always a continual stream of emotional information coming to you. In the beginning, it will just be easier to notice how you perceive emotional information if you do not need to make any important choices in that moment.

It would also be useful for you to become more aware of your surroundings, because you receive a great deal of emotional information externally, as well. Begin to notice the quality of the air around you. How does it feel? How does it smell? Is it moving or still? Does it feel dense or light? Begin to pay more attention to the animals and to the plants around you, as well. They are also constantly processing emotional information. Notice their choices, and dialogue with them about what they perceive. There is so much information available to you at all times, but it is up to you to become consciously aware of it.

Do emotions only exist in the third dimension, or are they part of the fifth-dimensional experience, as well?

Emotion is an aspect of both dimensional realities; however, you would not interpret emotional information fifth-dimensionally in the same ways that you do third-dimensionally. Experiencing emotion, making a choice, and manifesting consequences is third-dimensional. Experiencing emotion and accurately interpreting the information contained within the experience is fifth-dimensional. From a fifth-dimensional perspective, each emotion that you experience simply flows into another emotion, and that *is* the experience. Neither way is better or worse. They are just different. At the same time, understanding how to consciously engage with your emotional information feedback loop is a really important piece for you to have to be able to understand how to create reality from a fifth-dimensional perspective.

I have often heard the expression, "Feel your feelings." In this session, you have been using the expression, "Feel your emotions." What is the difference?

They are essentially the same thing. It is simply a matter of being aware that the human understanding of emotion is often judgmental. In reality, emotions cannot be individually named; collectively, they are simply information. It only becomes a specific emotion when you identify it as such. Naming and giving specific characteristics to emotions can only occur from a third-dimensional perspective.

But can't emotions sometimes lead you astray?

It is not the emotional information that is confusing you; it is the judgment about the emotion, and is due to your lack of experience in consciously engaging with your emotional information feedback loop. Emotional information is not static; it is in constant motion, like the wind. When you attempt to isolate a particular feeling, and name it, you completely miss the inherent information and make it into something else entirely. It is as if you attempt to cage the wind, and when it flows effortlessly out through the bars of your cage, you begin to analyze what is wrong with the wind. In order to accurately interpret emotional information, you must allow it to remain in context. Once you isolate it into a specific feeling, you change it. We hear you saying that you do not trust emotion, because emotion can lead you astray when, in fact, it is not the emotion that leads you astray; it is your reaction to your interpretation of the emotional information.

So is it what we initially do with the emotional information, when it first comes into our awareness, that determines what happens next? For example, if I feel angry and I judge it as bad, and then choose to feel guilty about feeling angry, have I misinterpreted the emotional information from the feeling of anger?

Exactly! Once you allow yourself to experience the feeling of anger, that piece of emotional information will move on, and you will be able to receive its message. Think about a time that you have cried yourself to sleep, and when you woke up, you felt better. Of course, you may have chosen to return to the original moment of when the emotional information had come into your awareness and begun crying again, but in that moment, you had the choice to see things differently. You know the saying, "Everything looks better in the light of day"? That saying comes from the fact that, with every new moment, you have the opportunity to choose to interpret your circumstances differently. There is always a lull after experiencing an intense emotion when you may suddenly have an understanding or a clarity that was not there before. That is a moment of choice.

I like to think of water as a metaphor for emotion, where I can either have a very still lake, or I can have huge waves. For me, emotion is more turbulent than a deep inner feeling of knowing.

The water is the emotional information, and the form it takes is your interpretation of it. When emotional information takes the form of a wave, it is still water. When you pull the emotional information into a wave and you call it anger, fear, joy, or whatever name you choose, you imagine that it freezes into place and stops moving. In reality, the wave falls back into the rest of the water, and in that moment, you again have the option to receive the emotional information, or you can name it again and create another wave.

As soon as you name an emotion and have a judgment about it, you are no longer in the present moment. Time has moved on, and you have chosen to remain in the past. You must remain in the present moment to be able to perceive reality fifth-dimensionally. You will only be able to see reality from a fifth-dimensional perspective when you are able to consciously engage with your emotional information feedback loop.

You currently perceive the continual flow of emotional information that you receive as being separate from your reality. It would be useful to suspend any judgment about this and instead look at how it serves you. Perhaps there are times in which the clutter in your garage causes you to be unable to accurately interpret any incoming emotional information and, consequently, it is a relief to disengage from the feedback loop for a while.

We suggest that you begin to become aware of when you are receptive to the emotional information feedback loop and when you are not, and notice the difference. What will inevitably happen is that you will recognize that consciously engaging with the emotional information feedback loop is more comfortable for you and, as a result, you will begin to make more choices that move you away from the fear end of the continuum and toward the love end. At this point, you are identifying most emotional information as overwhelming and choosing to consciously engage with it as little as possible. Once you begin to incorporate more love and less fear into your choices, it will become natural and instinctive for you to make choices from love. Making choices from love magnetically draws even more love into your energy field. We would like to now move into the meditation.

☸

Close your eyes and imagine that you are floating in space. It is a very safe feeling. It is like being in the womb. There is air and energy around you. It is not too dry. It is not too humid. You feel completely supported and completely weightless as you are floating there. Begin to notice something in the distance. It is coming toward you. It may be energy. It may be a color. It may be a geometrical shape. It may not be anything that you can identify. Just feel it moving toward you. It is not at all threatening. Notice that you are curious about what it is and why it is coming toward you. You can feel that it is also curious about you. Feel it slowly moving closer and closer to you and then join with you. You encompass it or it encompasses you; it does not matter. It is a pleasant sensation as you merge as one, just for an instant. It then moves beyond you. Notice what is different.

Now you are floating back in space again. You feel safe and very comfortable, very relaxed. Simply enjoy the sensation of weightlessly floating through space. Take a moment to notice what is different now. After a few minutes, notice again that there is something moving toward you. Feel its interest in you and your interest in it. Feel it move slowly toward you and merge with you, again, just for an instant. Feel how it changes you, and then feel it move on.

You are floating in space once again. Take a moment to notice what is different. Begin to notice that, yet again, something is being drawn toward you. Feel it move toward you. Feel yourself merge with it and feel yourself change as it passes through you. Then it is gone. The instant that it is gone, you notice that there is something else moving toward you. It is coming quicker this time and it merges with you, changes you, and moves on. Instantly, you realize that something else is out there and is being drawn toward you, even more quickly than before. Notice that there is always only one thing coming toward you at any given time, and recognize that it does not feel overwhelming. It is simply a continual flow that moves toward you, merges with you and moves on. Feel how each experience of merging changes your cellular makeup, and simultaneously notice that something else immediately catches your attention and is moving toward you.

Take a few minutes now and feel one after another move toward you and through you. If the movement begins to feel overwhelming, slow it down a little bit. Do not analyze them. Do not name them. Do not identify them. Do not try to decide if they are energy, color or a geometrical shape. Just feel them move toward you, merge with you and then move beyond you. As each one moves out of you, feel the next one moving into you.

Feel the waves of energy, and feel the unique sensations each time one moves through you. Feel how it replenishes you. Feel how you are becoming more of who you have always been. Feel your mind expanding. Feel your energy field filling with light. Notice that the light feels different than any light that you have experienced before. It is not something you see. It is something you feel deep within you. Recognize this as love, the creative energy of all that is. Recognize that it is coming from within you and without you and is around you, all at the same time. There is no separation between the empty space that you are floating in and that which you define as your energy field. Feel yourself merge with this wonderful energy full of sensory information.

Notice now that there is no distinct sensation of movement toward you, through you and beyond you. Notice that there is no differentiation. It is all you. Feel the vastness that you are. Feel the unlimited potential, the unlimited energy, the unlimited possibility that you are. Feel all that you believe to be possible expand exponentially, far beyond anything you ever envisioned until now. Know that your consciousness can reach out that far, and beyond, as of this moment.

See the vastness that you are flow into the vastness of something that is different than you are. Feel its curiosity about you and your curiosity about it. It is as vast as you are. Notice what happens as the vast experience of reality that you are, and that the other is, merge into each other. Feel the peace in that. Feel the rightness and the knowingness and the clarity in that union. You are safe and you are loved. You hold within you the divine spark of creation. You are loved by the very essence that is you, because it is you that is within you, and it is you that surrounds you. Feel the divinity that is within you.

Now, see yourself taking all that swirling divinity and pulling it back into the human form that you know yourself to be on earth in this time/space moment. Know that all that you have just experienced is contained within you. Know that you bring everything that you have just experienced back with you, and that you can consciously access it much easier than ever before. You have begun to remember all that you are. Everything that you do from this moment forth will come from the vastness of the love that you express within and around you.

When you are ready, slowly come back to this room and open your eyes. Know that you bring with you all that you have just experienced. Know that you are forever changed. We hold each of you, and that which each of you expresses, within our hearts. We love you more than you know.

Plants and Animals

"The plants and animals that you share your home with hold a magnetic attraction for you."

Are plants and animals going to ascend?

It is not really called ascension for them, because they do not operate under the veil of illusion that humans do. An inherent part of ascension is the recognition of your multidimensionality, and that has not been lost for plants and animals. Shortly before Earth ascends, it will seem as if all of the animals simply disappear. What actually happens to each species will differ based on choices made by each group.

Are there going to be plants and animals on the fifth-dimensional earth?

Oh, yes!

Will they be entirely new species?

It is not so much that they will be new species; it is more accurate to say that the species that you are currently aware of will be able to express more of who they are than they do now. At the same time, you will be able to recognize more of who they are because of your increased awareness. Although there is a whole continuum of awareness among plants and animals, the majority of them already operate multidimensionally. In fact, many of the plants and animals that are operating multidimensionally in this third dimension version of reality hold the possibility of ascension for us. It is as if there is an energy field generated by their multidimensional presence.

Let's use the garden outside as an example. Each of the plants that make up the garden are together generating a multidimensional holographic energy field. That field is made up of the combined energy of all the plants in the garden. While it is natural for this to happen from the perspective of the plants, it also serves as a vibrational reminder of what is possible for humans as humans become increasingly aware that individuality is an illusion. Multidimensional awareness cannot be experienced individually; it has to happen in groups. We do not mean groups that gather in the same location, like this one; we mean soul groups.

Ascension is not an individual experience. Although the choice to move into ascension appears to be an individual choice, remember that experiencing yourself as individual can only happen from a third-dimensional perspective. It is essential that you be consciously connected to the energy of the other Beings in your soul group to experience ascension. Each group of plants and/or animals generates a unique energetic field, as does each human soul group. There is not one ascension process; rather, there are an infinite number of ways in which ascension can be experienced. You do not need to worry about finding your soul group, because you will naturally be energetically drawn to them and instantly recognize them.

Can plants and animals be part of your soul group?

Certainly, although they play different roles than the human members do. The role of the plants and animals can be compared to the quiet, slow-burning embers of a fire that might appear to have burned itself out. The fire in this analogy represents the energy of multidimensional awareness that the plants and animals emanate for you while you completely immerse yourselves in this illusionary experience. Because they hold that energy, you are unable to entirely forget your divinity. Remember that part of being multidimensional is being able to consciously manifest in various forms, and consider the possibility that when you perceive the form of a particular animal, that form is merely one of infinite possible manifestations of that Being.

Just as you are energetically drawn to other humans in your

soul group, you are also drawn to particular species of plants and animals. The plants and animals that you share your home with hold a magnetic attraction for you, and aligning with their vibration is a key to remembering who you are. As we have said before, ascension is not something you have to learn how to do; it is merely a matter of remembering how it feels. When you are within an energetic field created by plants or animals, your innate cellular encoding for ascension is activated.

Your connection to the plants and animals reminds you of the group consciousness that you were part of in Lemuria. Becoming consciously aware of this communication is a necessary step in the ascension process. As you move through the ascension process, you automatically reconnect to everyone in your soul group, and your unique vibration begins to hum within each of their energy fields, and at the same time, their energetic signature vibrates within you. It is important to understand that 'within' is not a location; it is an inclusion.

Communication is the key to ascension. It is only from a third-dimensional perspective that communication can break down between individuals or groups of individuals. Polarity cannot exist when you no longer create your reality under the illusion of separation. As you become more aware of your connection to all beings and begin to consciously participate in the ongoing energy exchange that exists between you, you will inevitably become aware of how what you are creating affects everything in your reality.

You must descend into in order to ascend. You must be here as consciously as possible to facilitate the changes that you desire. If you have not taken full responsibility for your creation of this reality, then you have skipped the first step in the ascension process. Consciously reconnecting with the plants and animals is a great way to descend, because they provide a buffer between the harshness of the third dimension and the divinity that you are innately yearning to express. You cannot move any further into conscious ascension energy until you become fully aware of your creative potential and recognize that which you are already creating third-dimensionally.

Everything you need to become a consciously ascended Being is right in front of you. Many of you have been doing everything you can to barely be here. You merely tolerate this reality while longing to go "home." We are here to tell you that you *are* home. You are bringing the energy that you call home into the physical forms in which you currently reside, and you have provided yourself with all the elements necessary to make that happen. With the slightest shift in your perception of what you call home, and through your connection with the plants and animals, you can begin to recognize that which is already within you.

We will give you an example. Imagine that you are sitting in meditation and ask for spiritual support regarding an issue that you are struggling with, and your dog comes into the room and nuzzles you. You meant to close the door and you are annoyed at the interruption, so you push the dog away and say, "Get out of here. I am meditating." Your dog was offering the support you were asking for, but because you had a preconceived idea of what you needed, you rejected the very assistance that you had just requested. As another example: you know that the weeds are taking over your garden, but you decide that do not have time to weed today, because you are feeling ungrounded and hope that you will feel better if you meditate. So you choose to meditate and do not weed your garden. Yet, when you have finished meditating, you don't feel any better, because what you really needed was to spend time in the energy of your garden.

It no longer serves you to create a spiritual life that is separate from your everyday life. They need to become one and the same. Everything that you do must be experienced with the same reverence that you invoke during meditation, and every meditation must be seen as merely another aspect of that which you perceive to be your third-dimensional reality. It is imperative that you consciously engage with each and every moment. As it is now, you spend a considerable amount of time in stasis. By stasis, we mean that you stop consciously engaging with the life energy that is all around you.

You must begin to pay more attention to what you are doing at all times. When you recognize that you have been unconscious for a moment, reengage with the current moment through your senses. Begin externally. Notice what it smells like. Feel the temperature of the air around you. Become aware of the sounds. Then move your awareness to your internal self. Notice your thoughts, your emotions, and how you are experiencing your physical body. Take a breath and notice all the assistance that wants to support you as you move into ascension.

Ascension is not a goal; it is an experience. We do not want you to become attached to our terminology of ascension as a process with specific steps, because that is not technically accurate. It is a little bit misleading when we refer to descending as the first step. It is more a matter of being able to consciously function within more levels of vibration simultaneously. It can be compared to when astronauts in the space program are trained in stages to effectively and comfortably do their jobs without the familiar sensations of gravity.

Conscious ascension, in the way that you are doing it, has never been done before. Because of that, you have to allow your physical vehicle to acclimate to increasing levels of light and energy as you move further into ascension. You cannot do it all at once or you will move beyond physicality. Consider the possibility that some of the issues that seem to be holding you back from expressing a higher degree of divine expression are literally anchoring you here in this reality. You are part of the advance team. You are individually and collectively working out the kinks of conscious ascension so that you can assist others as they move through ascension in the future.

Does that explain why working with flower essences is helpful?

When you work with essences, you are working with the energy of the plants multidimensionally. Working with essences brings the specific vibration of that plant to assist you. You do not actually need a manifested version of the essence to receive the desired assistance, but working with essences third-dimensionally allows a physical touchstone that helps you repeatedly bring your conscious intention into the process.

How does what you are saying apply to plant and animal allergies?

Any time that you have an allergic reaction to something on a physical level, it is resistance to an aspect of the energetic vibration of that particular plant or animal. Basically, when an energetic vibration that you are unable to assimilate enters your energy field, you essentially create a block or a filter to resist the energy. Physically, you experience this as an allergic reaction. However, any vibrational energy that comes into your energetic field is there for a reason, and it is up to you to be willing to accept what is being offered. The reason that allergies often worsen over time is due to the fact that people begin to identify the allergen as the problem; this, in turn, elicits an emotional response of frustration, anger and/or helplessness that compounds the resistance already being experienced.

What can we do to work through our allergic reactions?

You can envision the energy of whatever it is you are reacting to and ask what is being offered to you through that form. You can also do a little bit of research about that plant or animal to learn the metaphysical properties it represents. Secondly, you can make a conscious effort to stop resisting what you are allergic to. Instead of reacting to it, begin engaging with the vibrational energy of that plant or animal. We do not suggest that, initially, you do this physically. Instead, call to you an image or a sensation of whatever you are having an allergic reaction to, and notice how you react physically, mentally and emotionally. Ask for an understanding of what is being offered. Working with the energy of the plant or animal in essence form, as well as using homeopathic remedies to work with the emotional aspects of the allergies, is also useful.

Is it because of their multidimensionality that animals are able to live in the now?

There is nothing other than the present moment for both plants and animals. That being said, animals sometimes move out of the eternal now to take on the disease or the emotions of the people that they live with. Animals are sometimes willing to move into the third-dimensional illusion to assist a human. It is not a difficult decision for them.

Are plants and animals part of a group energy?

Each species of plant and animal is a group in and of itself.

Do plants or animals ever individuate?

It might appear that they individuate when they choose to move into the third dimension to assist a human, but they never completely lose connection to their group soul. It is their group connection that allows them to move into the third dimension. This is true for humans, as well, which is what we were talking about earlier in regard to the importance of conscious reconnection with your soul group.

Plants and animals allow themselves to be drawn into the third dimension to remind humans of their divine potential. We are including wild animals in this, as well. Look at how many people focus on the energy of wolves when the debate about their reintroduction becomes headline news in particular areas.

Are houseplants affected more by human contact than plants outside?

Although individual houseplants may seem to be more isolated than outdoor plants because they are in pots and unable to connect to other plants through the soil, they are still able to connect with each other etherically. They connect with each other through the energy of the sun in an ongoing energetic exchange. Plants use the sun as a satellite and continually send their energetic vibration into the sun, and that vibration is then beamed down into other plants. In a natural setting, the part of the plant that lives above ground is energetically connected to other plants via the sun, as well as within the soil through their root system. So, while indoor plants, without their root systems being connected to the earth, are not completely separated energetically from other plants, they must connect with the energy around the pot that they are planted in. As a result, indoor plants are often more in tune with the human energetic vibrations that continually move through the air than are outdoor plants.

I find that to communicate with a dog that I am working with, I actually have to go through her soul group...

It would be useful for you to communicate with the dog in terms of her person, because the issues that you are addressing are coming from the dog's person, and that perspective would make more sense to the dog. You are attempting to communicate with the dog as an individual, and she does not perceive herself individually. Although she is aware of her connection to her soul group, she sees her current role as being in service to her person.

It is important to understand that, like humans, plants and animals have evolved over time. It would be useful for you to remember how plants, animals and humans related to each other in Lemuria, Atlantis and Egypt. This will give you an idea of how you will all communicate with each other in the future. In Atlantis, for example, dogs were considered to be very regal Beings.

While is not entirely accurate to say that they were rare, there was not the overabundance of dogs that exists today. There were not rabid dogs running through the streets in Atlantis. They were either valued in esteemed positions, or they were not there at all. There were not litters of dogs born unwanted; they did not have animal shelters in Atlantis. There was no need. Part of the reason there is currently such an abundance of some animals, both domestic and wild, is due to the unconsciousness of humans. In effect, they are overly abundant in order to offer as much of their energy as possible in any given moment.

Is that true of plants, too?

Yes, many of which you call weeds.

Does that mean that knapweed has come here to hold a certain consciousness for us?

Absolutely. Knapweed is here to remind you to be conscious, because if you are not, it begins to fill in everything that you are not conscious about. You have to be clear where you do not want knapweed, and take action to make it not be there. The presence of knapweed offers you the opportunity to practice being in the moment and clarifying what you want and/or don't want. With knapweed, there are certain times when it is less work to get it under control. For example, if you destroy it in the spring, it requires very little effort to keep it at bay for the rest of the summer. This is also the case in your own process, as there are more and less potent times in your personal creation cycles.

Is there a way of working with knapweed to get it to leave a certain area without killing it using poisons and chemicals?

Knapweed, as a species, is very good at survival. If it is not allowed to take root on your property, it will find another place where it is tolerated. It is not your responsibility to ensure that knapweed will perpetuate itself; it can do that on its own. It would be useful for you to consider the presence of knapweed as an opportunity to practice standing up for what you want, or in this case, don't want, in your literal physical environment. It is this same certainty that you must transfer to the creation of your spiritual, mental and emotional realities. Do not confuse respect for the knapweed in terms of its right to exist with allowing it to flourish at the expense of your gardens and lawns. Be very clear on what you do and do not want to be part of your experience, and then don't be afraid to take a stand. That is the message of knapweed.

Knapweed cannot be negotiated with. You must be very clear on the fact that it is not welcome, and you must take whatever steps necessary to eliminate it. How you choose to eliminate the knapweed is not as important as are your reasons for wanting to eliminate it. While it is true that you can relate to some plants telepathically, there are others that are not interested in your perspective. They are here for their own reasons, and the human point of view is irrelevant to them. You want the knapweed to be gone, yet you feel guilty about having that desire, so you temper how you go about eliminating it. From the perspective of knapweed, it is either welcome or it is not welcome. There is no in-between. If you create or allow a hospitable environment for it to grow, it will, and if you don't, it won't. It is that simple.

The same is true for what you choose to include in your life. In order to create the kind of experience that you are striving for, you need to choose what you do and do not want to be part of your reality, and your actions need to be consistent with those choices. What many of you do instead is be indiscriminately inclusive about whom and what you incorporate into your life, and then wonder why so many problems and conflicts arise for you. It is important that you become more conscious about what you choose to include and exclude by the choices that you make and the relationships that you choose to cultivate.

Can you talk more about how we can communicate with the plants that are receptive to telepathic communication from humans?

Many of you already talk to trees. What you may not understand is that it is not only a two-way conversation. It is, in fact, a group conversation that includes the ground you are standing on, the bird sitting on a branch of the tree, the lichen growing on its bark, and the grass beneath you. It is not so much a matter of learning how to communicate with the natural world around you as it is learning to interpret the ongoing conversations that are already taking place. The key to being able to consciously communicate with the natural world is to get used to simultaneously participating in multiple conversations. If you were in a room in which everyone was talking at the same time, at first it might be difficult to understand anyone. Initially, you might need to choose which conversations you were most interested in, and tune out all of the others so that you could begin to make sense of some of what was being said. This is the same technique that you can use to begin to consciously communicate with plants and animals.

What currently happens is that when you set the intention that you want to communicate with plants or animals, your conscious awareness immediately shifts, but as you tune into the cacophony of conversation that is happening around you, you become overwhelmed, because you are not used to the intensity of it. Your awareness then contracts again and your interpretation is that nothing happened, and you conclude you are unable to communicate with plants and animals.

Just as you would in a room full of people, you need to focus on a particular element of the conversation; in this case, a specific plant or animal. Once you are able to begin communicating with them, you can incorporate another plant or animal into the conversation and so on. In this way, you can gradually expand your awareness of communication between yourself and the natural world.

There are two important aspects for you to understand that will help you with this. The first is to not expect the communication from plants and animals to come in the form of words. Telepathic communication takes place much more quickly than do verbal conversations, and involve conveying all aspects of a thought in a split second, including, but not limited to, the sensory aspects. This is what often trips humans up. Even though the entire thought has already been conveyed from the plant or animal, the human is still trying to decipher the first word. It can be compared to the human playing charades, i.e.: three words, first letter, first word, et cetera, and the plant or animal is playing a virtual reality video game. If you are not playing the same game, it just won't work.

The second aspect that will be helpful for you to consider is the fact that you perceive the plant or animal that you desire to communicate with as separate from yourself. For example, you perceive yourself to be in human form and the tree before you to be in plant form. This is directly relevant to how you attempt to communicate with it. You try to figure out how to translate your words into a language that the tree will understand. The underlying assumption is that you speak different languages. Consider the possibility that it is not so much that you are different species as it is that you are different manifestations of the same energetic vibration, and as such, inherently speak the same language. You don't have to learn how to do this. You just have to remember that you already know how to do this. It is through remembering your connection to everything around you that you will be able to communicate with plants and animals.

How do fairies and devas fit in with what we are talking about?

Fairies and devas are part of the elemental kingdom. Elemental Beings function as translators or messengers. Their main job is to support the various dimensional realities that simultaneously exist at any given time. Elemental Beings are essential to the existence of seemingly incompatible multidimensional perceptions of reality. These Beings contain the blueprints of those with whom they work, and are constantly adjusting energy forms to allow them to exist in whichever dimensional reality they choose and to tune out those realities that they choose not to be aware of. It can be compared to the way that an antenna works to tune in the reception of a television, or the tracking device on a VCR. The elemental Beings are often required to fill in energetic gaps in the matrixes, which, if left open, would cause the illusionary realities to disintegrate.

The elemental Beings coordinate the fundamental framework of all expressed realities. When you desire a particular manifestation, it is the elemental Beings that make it happen. There are an infinite number of elemental Beings working behind the scenes at any given moment. Each of you has a personal network of elemental Beings who work incessantly to orchestrate your chosen version of reality.

From some perspectives, it would appear that the gridlines around the planet are made up of these Beings; however, it is not that they reside within the grid itself. It is more accurate to say that it is their consciousness that holds the grid in place. Another way of thinking about it is that the elemental Beings generate the energetic vibration that makes up the matrix itself, and it is human consciousness that chooses how the matrix is configured in any given moment. Although it is the matrix that creates the third-dimensional illusion and allows you to exist in human form, you must understand that it is your consciousness that creates the matrix. Each individual choice affects the matrix, and the energetic vibration reflected through the elementals into the matrix at any given moment becomes a crystallization of the collective choices, which, in turn, generates new possible templates of reality that then present new choices—and the cycle continues.

It is useful to think about the matrix as a work in progress that is reaching completion. Once the matrix is complete, the elemental Beings will no longer be needed to generate the vibrational energy to create the matrix. At that time, it will essentially become a version of reality that is energetically sustained differently. This process can be compared to a paper mache project.

In paper mache, newspaper strips and glue are layered onto a balloon in the shape of that which you want to create. In this analogy, the balloon represents the original intention, and the air inside the balloon is being generated by the elemental Beings.

Once you adhere several layers of the glue and newspaper strips onto the balloon, you can pop the balloon and still have a solid form that retains the shape that was being held by the balloon. This is what is currently taking place as individuals are choosing to fully descend in preparation for conscious ascension. It is the desire to manifest a particular version of reality, as defined by collective intention, that gives form to what is manifested. Returning to our analogy, once your paper mache form solidifies, you are able to decorate it as you wish. This can be compared to the conscious creation as you move into ascension. Decorating the solidified form represents the new multidimensional version of reality being created by human consciousness.

As we have said before, it is only when human Beings choose to consciously descend into third-dimensional reality that they are able to consciously move into ascension. It is the manifestation of third-dimensional reality through human consciousness that allows ascension to occur. Just as the balloon that originally holds the shape of what is being created in paper mache appears to be much less concrete than does the final product, the final product could not have come into existence without the balloon.

What will happen to the elemental Beings when Earth ascends?

When Earth ascends, if a Being chooses to remain in the form of an elemental, they will go on to create a matrix somewhere else. It is also a possibility that they will choose a different form, since all Beings have the same options available to them that you do in terms of which form each of you chooses to manifest as.

I have another question about animals. I have gone through several severe illnesses, and each time, one of my animals has experienced the same illness that I was going through. Can you explain that?

There is a lot of energy involved by the time you manifest an illness, and sometimes animals choose to assist you through the process by taking on some of that energy themselves. An animal would not manifest illness for any other reason. It serves no purpose from their perspective. Once you have this awareness, it does not serve you or them to feel guilty. This will not resolve the issue at hand. What is needed is for you to take responsibility for what is manifesting in your physicality in the form of illness and through your animals, and to identify and alter the core belief systems that are being played out within your life. Depending on your relationship with the animal, sometimes you can ask them to help you identify the issue.

Can we call upon the elemental kingdom for assistance in healing?

Yes, but keep in mind that elemental Beings are very no-nonsense and do not respond to emotion. If you are not sincerely committed to the change that you are asking them to make, do not be surprised if they are unwilling to assist you. Do not expect to have a long conversation with them about your request. From their perspective, either you want to be in balance or you don't. The elemental Beings consider your choices as clear indicators of what you want, regardless of any conflicting emotions that you may be experiencing about it yourself. That being said, if you are truly committed to moving into balance, you can ask for their assistance. Then, get out of the way and allow them to do their job. They are quick and efficient, and whatever you have requested will be addressed immediately.

Why don't they just help us without us asking for help?

Free will is a fundamental aspect of this version of reality, and as such, they are not allowed to interfere with your choices without your permission. Any illness that you manifest is a result of your choices, and to interfere would invalidate your free will. Their job is to keep the overall reality in balance, and if you are personally out of balance, they simply work around you.

Do animals experience feelings and emotions in the same way that we do?

It is possible for animals to experience emotions as humans do, but it is only through their connection to humans that animals experience emotion at all. Once an animal expands its understanding to include a particular human-related emotional experience, that emotional information, and what is elicited as a result of the experience from both the animal's and the human's perspective, becomes part of, and permanently alters, their understanding of reality.

Is it the same with plants?

Plants are similar to elementals in regard to emotional energy, although plants would be considered logical where elementals are efficient. If you were to think in terms of an emotional continuum, animals would be at one end, with elementals on the opposite end, and plants in the middle. Like animals, plants experience emotional energy as information, and then make logical choices without regard for the humans involved one way or the other. Think back to our discussion of knapweed as an example of the logic of plants.

Have we bred a degree of consciousness out of animals to get them to be domesticated?

It would be more accurate to say that some species of animals have agreed to forgo many of their natural instincts in order to interact more closely with humans. Humans, as a species, do not have the power to make choices for any other species. However, agreements have been made between some species of animals and humans for the sole purpose of experiencing themselves individually and collectively from a different perspective.

Do some animals, like cows for example, retain less conscious awareness when they make this choice?

Sometimes they do. It is a continuum. For example, most of the cows that are not meant to be eaten, such as dairy cows, are at one end of the continuum and retain full consciousness of their third-dimensional experience, whereas cows that are bred solely for consumption are at the other end of the continuum and retain very little conscious awareness of their experience. Cows that live on large, mechanical dairies and rarely have contact with humans will have less consciousness than cows that are allowed to roam freely and develop a connection to humans. You might want to take the degree of consciousness present in your food products into consideration and pay more attention to where what you consume originates.

That being said, consuming food with little or no energy does not, in and of itself, cause you any harm. Although you can choose the quality of energy to ingest, the determining factor that affects how the energy of what you eat is assimilated into your body depends on what you think about what you eat, not what you actually eat. It is what you believe about what you eat that is converted into energy.

Is it possible to transmute the energy of food before we eat it?

That is an option, but when you do that, the result is neutral. Essentially, what happens is that you choose to eat something that you believe to have a low vibration. You then transmute some of your higher vibration into the food and proceed to eat it. Look at what happens: you are simply consuming energy that was already part of you. Logically, it does not make a lot of sense to do it that way. Consider the possibility that it is not through its ostensible energetic value that food energetically replenishes you. We suggest that you take into consideration the ways in which eating feeds you, other than nutritionally. For example, think about what you gain when you choose to eat that which you might call "comfort foods." Imagine how much more energetically beneficial it would be if you gave yourself permission to eat that type of food without experiencing guilt.

Can you explain why cows are choosing to manifest Mad Cow Disease?

Cows, as a species, have chosen to phase themselves out of human reality. In essence, the cows are unwilling to participate any longer in the roles that they play for humans overall. Cows consider the manifestation of Mad Cow Disease to be a way in which they can contribute to raising human consciousness.

Is that the same with dolphins and pods of whales that beach themselves?

In some cases, yes.

Are there some species of animals that will leave the planet before 2012, when Earth herself ascends?

Oh yes, many. It is already happening. If you want to know which ones, just take a look at the endangered species list.

I have also heard that new species will be emerging. Is this true?

There will be entirely new species that move into physicality, as well as the return of some species that are currently considered to be extinct and others that are only believed to be myths. A template of all animals interested in interacting with humans at any point along the time/space continuum of this third-dimensional illusionary version of reality perpetually exists beyond the limits of typical human senses, and they, as a group, choose when to manifest and when to recede into the world beyond form.

As an example, at some point dolphins may choose to leave physicality altogether and interact only etherically with humans. There are many of you who yearn to be with the dolphins. If you are drawn to the energy of the dolphins, then you are already deeply connected to them, and we suggest that you release your attachment to the idea that you have to physically be with them to experience that connection. Practice feeling them and communicating with them right now, regardless of how far from them you may live. Connecting with dolphin energy offers you the opportunity to become familiar with what it feels like to be ethereal while you are still in physicality. It is a wonderful way to consciously experience yourself from a multidimensional perspective. In the following meditation, we will give you a few ways that you can consciously tune into their energetic vibrations.

☸

Begin by focusing on any plant or animal that you would like to communicate with and say out loud, "I would like to become consciously aware of that which is within me that appears to be without." The effect of this will be that the imagined separation between you and the plant or animal that you desire to connect with will immediately dissolve, and the channels of communication between you will open up. Keep in mind that the communication will consist of emotions, images and sudden understandings. Telepathic communication is not made up of single words and sentences, but of entire pictures or stories.

It may initially feel overwhelming and confusing; it might seem as if many conversations are taking place simultaneously. This does not mean that you will literally hear them talking to you, or even see the actual images being communicated to you. It is more likely that you will be using senses beyond the five that humans usually use. Simply allow yourself to sense what is happening. Don't try too hard. Relax into the experience.

In the beginning, we suggest that you do this for only a few minutes at a time, and then go about your normal business. You don't even need to attempt to communicate back right away. This way, you are able to tune into what is being communicated without engaging with it through your conscious mind. Tuning into the natural world around you will be a few moments of relaxation, as opposed to something that you have to work at. If you try too hard, you will miss the subtleness of what is happening. It will be useful to initially focus on being receptive. This will help you "be" instead of "do," and is a fundamental aspect of telepathic communication.

Keep in mind that it is not always necessary to specifically identify where the communication is coming from. For example, if you are sitting in a garden doing this exercise, you do not need to know the name of each plant that is connecting with you. With practice, you will be able to identify individual voices, but in the beginning, it will only serve to engage your analytical mind and distract you from the sensory nature of telepathic communication.

The same is true for communication with animals. You may intend to connect to a squirrel that you see in a tree, and instead, begin conversing with a caterpillar that you are not aware is even there. Just go with it. It is likely that the tree and the grass below your feet may also join in the conversation. Remember that all elements of the natural world are connected multidimensionally and do not perceive themselves as individual.

☸

Attuning to the energy of plants and animals is quite useful in terms of expanding your multidimensional awareness, and we suggest that you make it a point to connect with the natural world around you for a few moments at least once each day.

The Time/Space Continuum

"It takes the conscious awareness of realities converging to recognize that what you call reality is only an illusion."

What is the purpose of the time/space continuum?

Time/space is unique to the third dimension. The time/space continuum is an idea that was conceived as part of the third-dimensional illusion in order for Beings to experience the intricacies of manifesting reality. A significant component of a third-dimensional experience is that reality is manifested through a three-step process involving intention, action and consequence. In order for this sequence to be perceived as three separate steps, there needs to be the illusion of time between each of them. Each dimensional reality has its own rules that must be followed in order for the illusion of that reality to manifest.

The concept of time/space can be difficult to think about because you are quite entrenched in a third-dimensional illusion in which one of the basic components is the concept of time/space. The challenge is to find ways to define yourself and the reality in which you are participating without using time/space as a given component of your definition. You need to be able to think about the theory of time/space, and at the same time, recognize that it is a completely intrinsic part of yourself. It can be compared to expecting a fish to understand that the very water that sustains it is not real, and to instead conceptualize it in an abstract fashion, rather than as an intrinsic element required for its existence. This session will be a study in existentialism.

We are going to discuss the concept of time/space from a variety of different perspectives, and each angle will provide you with another facet to your understanding of it. When you leave, some of you may feel more confused than when you arrived. Trust that the information that doesn't make sense to your mind will be stored in your energy field and will be available to you at a later time, when you step into full awareness of who you are. There is going to be a moment of clarity for each of you as you are able to momentarily get past your cognitive understanding and are able to conceptualize with full awareness how fundamental time/space is to everything that you perceive as real.

Can you give us an example of what time/space isn't a part of?

When you are dreaming, you are operating beyond the illusion of time/space. Think about how you can be in one place in a dream and then, suddenly, you are able to be somewhere else in an instant, even though you didn't actually move. The place itself changes. That is one example of what can't happen in time/space based reality. Another aspect of dreams is that things can occur out of sequence. Dreams are a really good way to conceptualize not participating in the illusion of time/space. Think about what you are able to do in dreams, and try those same things when you are awake. Imagine how fun that could be! In the coming months, it is going to be more difficult to distinguish when you are awake and when you are dreaming. It will be useful for you to consider engaging with reality at all times as if you are dreaming.

Does that mean that during the night our bodies would be resting, and during the day, we would be dreaming... like the Aborigines?

As it is now, your bodies are not so much resting at night as they are traveling and gathering information. Because time/space is not a fundamental aspect in dreams, you are able to experience multiple realities at the same time while you are dreaming. When you wake up and remember a dream, you are only remembering what can be conceptualized third-dimensionally. There were actually many other realities that you were participating in, and aware of, in your dream state. Soon, you are going to be able to bring the concept of multiple realities into your consciousness while you are awake, as well.

You have not been able to do this until now because the wiring in your brain wasn't activated to do so, but that has changed as you have moved further into conscious awareness. You have received an upgrade in your hard wiring that will be helpful for you to be able to comprehend the idea of multiple realities. The difference is that information will no longer come only through your mind. Instead, it will come to you in a variety of ways. Your mind is what has assisted you in perpetuating the illusion of this third-dimensional reality, and it will be useful for you to begin to distinguish between when information is being filtered through your mind and when it comes to you in other ways.

You are in the habit of perceiving what comes through your mind as a definitive perspective of reality, and it is going to take a little bit of practice to get used to noticing that there are multiple perspectives of everything that you experience. Eventually, you will be able to recognize when your mind is engaging with one version of reality and other parts of you are simultaneously engaging with alternative versions of the same reality.

How do our experiences of sometimes having tremendous amounts of energy, and then other times having absolutely no energy, relate to the concept of time/space?

Sometimes when you are experiencing low energy, information is being downloaded into your energy field and you need extra energy to assimilate it. At other times, you may be participating in another reality, and a large part of your consciousness is temporarily more focused on that other reality than on this one. Because the part of you that chooses where to delegate your energy knows what is happening in both realities, you can trust that your energy is needed more there than here and allow yourself to take it easy until you feel your energy return. On the other hand, sometimes if what you are doing in this reality is the priority, you will experience lots of energy and feel exceptionally creative. Until you recognize the degree to which you operate within the illusion of time/space, you will continue to experience these low and high points in your energy.

So it is not necessarily a bad thing if you feel low energy?

No, not at all, but when you do experience times of low energy, the best thing you can do for yourself is to go to sleep or to just sit on the couch and read or watch TV. Sometimes what is happening elsewhere involves your mind, and sometimes it doesn't. When you are experiencing low energy, pay attention to how it is affecting you. Are you physically tired? Are you emotionally tired? Are you mentally tired? Then allow that aspect or aspects of yourself to rest. Sometimes, you may need to go to sleep. Other times, you would actually be better off doing something physical that doesn't involve a lot of mental energy, like going for a walk or working out. Simply determine what you need, and then address the identified need, knowing that you are facilitating something that is important for another aspect of yourself.

You are going to have to make some choices. For example, if you have made a commitment to be somewhere and you don't have the energy to get out of bed, there are going to be consequences if you choose not to honor your commitment. In this situation, it would be useful for you to recognize that if someone gets angry with you, or if you don't make money because you don't go to work, that you are choosing to make your process a priority. You will have to develop an element of trust here.

This new way of participating in reality is going to take some practice, because all of your false illusions are going to be called to your attention, and you are going to have the opportunity to reevaluate them. Sometimes, it might feel like you are not holding it all together anymore. In fact, that will be true, but that is simply because you are not meant to hold this illusionary reality together anymore. It is time to expand out into a broader perspective of reality beyond time/space.

Once you get the hang of this and look back on one of those days when you chose to stay in bed instead of going to work, you will be able to see that what was important that day was maybe a meeting in the future version of Atlantis at which you were the key speaker. These are the kind of situations that you are simultaneously participating in all the time; you are simply not yet aware of that fact from your current perspective. Set the intention to always operate from your highest integrity and trust what happens, and suspend the judgment that you are being irresponsible. You are going to have to rethink this whole idea of commitment to other people, because from this point on, you must make moving into conscious awareness your highest priority. Otherwise, if you continue to make the current reality your focus, you will be unable to move your consciousness into the emerging reality. Remember, it is your choices that manifest the reality that you experience.

We suggest that, as often as possible, you don't make definite plans, because you can't be sure of what you are going to need from moment to moment. An example of one way to go about this is that if someone wants to make dinner plans with you, express your interest and agree to decide the afternoon before you plan to go to dinner. Certainly keep your options open, but make it clear to people not to make any plans around you. If you would like to make it easy on yourself, let everyone in your life know that this is the new way you are going to be making plans, and that you are not going to commit to anything for a while.

Each of you has a built-in radar of what is yours to do, and all that is required is that you pay attention to it. When you don't pay attention to it, you become sick or find yourself in a relationship that is uncomfortable or at a job that you don't like. When you realize that you are doing something that is having physical or emotional repercussions, carefully decide if you want to continue to choose it. Recognize that you are creating your reality by the choices that you make in each moment.

Begin to practice letting go of planning so much of your life, and begin small. Start doing this on a weekend when you don't have as many obligations. Decide not to make any plans one Saturday, and see where the weekend takes you. When you get the hang of that, try it on a Monday and see where the week takes you. It is not our intention to encourage you to be irresponsible when we make these suggestions. For instance, if you choose not to go to work one day or choose not to honor a commitment that you have made, and then wake up the following day and don't want to get out of bed because you would prefer to avoid dealing with the consequences of your choice, that is not following your heart. Each choice that you make must be made with integrity.

As you begin to practice following your heart, there may be times that you recognize that what you are committed to is not what you truly want to be doing. That is okay. Honor your agreements, and at the same time, be aware of the choices that you are making. Then, gradually begin to make fewer commitments and leave more unscheduled time on your calendar. Begin to become comfortable with living moment-to-moment. Making plans in this way brings a high degree of authenticity to everything that you do.

Are you saying that when we are experiencing really high energy, we are more fully participating in this reality?

Sometimes, yes. You may be doing something here that has been prioritized as being where most of your energy needs to be in that moment. It could also be that your consciousness is not needed elsewhere, and you have an opportunity to experience what it is like to be fully conscious in this reality in the present moment.

Are the Beings that created time/space available to work with us? Can they help adjust our circuitry so that this transition will be less difficult?

Your circuitry is already being adjusted, because that is what has set this transition process into motion. It is only your resistance to changing your perception about what you call reality that makes the process feel difficult. With that in mind, you can always ask for the process to be slowed down so that you can have more time to adjust, if you wish. For example, if your belief is that you really do need to go to work on a particular day, ask for the energy to do so, and schedule a time on your calendar when you can spend a couple of days at home without any commitments. You can always negotiate with yourself if you need to. However, we suggest that you always examine your motivation before renegotiating. For example, do you need to go to work because the regional manager is making his monthly visit today and you have a great idea to present to him, or because you are worried that if you take a day off, you won't be able to buy groceries this month?

It is of utmost importance that you do not repeatedly put off allowing yourself the needed downtime. Since you have made the choice to set this process into motion, you will eventually have to allow your body to make the needed changes. The times of low energy that you experience are chosen with your best interest in mind. If you can simply trust that all the details will work themselves out and allow yourself to rest, it will be far less difficult for you in the end.

How do changes in the time/space continuum affect the aging process?

Aging and dying have always been a choice, and the choice to participate in the illusion of aging is independent from choosing to participate in the illusion of time/space. However, the two illusions do work well together. Your bodies are adjusting proportionately as the time/space illusion is collapsing upon itself, so it will not cause you to age faster, even if you are still participating in the illusion that aging is inevitable. Just think about how much faster time passes now than it did when you were younger. It is not an inevitable facet of getting older, as you believe it to be. It is because time is actually speeding up. Although it appears to be happening in conjunction with you getting older, that is only because you believe there to be a correlation between the two illusions.

It seems to me that dreamtime is more fourth-dimensional and motivated by our feelings, and fifth-dimensional manifestation is motivated by desire or inspiration and can manifest beyond past, present or future. I have noticed that when I have a project I need to do, that to plan it out in the third dimension feels very tedious, but then I feel a ball of energy around me, and something shifts, and I become motivated and inspired.

The ball of energy that you refer to is your Merkaba. When you are in your Merkaba, you are simultaneously operating beyond time/space and within a time/space experience. The fourth dimension is actually experienced as a continuum. When you are working within the fourth dimension closer to the third-dimensional end, you operate more within the time/space illusion. You need to understand that there are varying degrees of time/space that can be incorporated into an illusionary reality. For example, lucid dreaming is roughly three-fourths of the way along the fourth-dimensional continuum perception of time/space toward the fifth-dimensional end. Keep in mind that this is a linear way to talk about dimensional manifestation. In reality, it is not a linear concept.

This is why playing with reality in dreams gives you a sense of both fifth-dimensional and third-dimensional manifestation and allows you to move in and out of both dimensional realities. The goal right now is not immediate ascension. What you are experimenting with is being able to consciously incorporate multidimensional awareness into your third-dimensional experience. This is an entirely new way of experiencing ascension and is referred to as 'conscious ascension.' Many of you are going to be teaching other Beings about conscious ascension in the future and are just now in the process of working out the kinks. Once you move through the process yourselves, you can offer future waves of Beings moving into conscious ascension tools and techniques to make it easier for them.

You are the perfect candidates to do this, because this third-dimensional experience is very dear to you, and you are not yet ready to completely move out of it. It is essential that you share with others this great love that you have for this experience. In part, it is the love that you have for earth, but it is also the love that you have for each other and what you have created here together. In an earlier question, someone referred to the creators of time; you need to realize that you are those very creators. For lack of a better way to explain it, imagine that one day, you all sat around a table and drew up the blueprint of this reality. Each one of you then took on the responsibility of manifesting the different aspects of your plan.

What can we do to assist ourselves in moving our consciousness beyond the illusion of time and space?

Becoming consciously aware of how habitual you are will help you begin to recognize how you experience your world based on the concepts of time and space. It is a fundamental component of existing within a third-dimensional illusionary reality that you limit the level of information that you are able to process with the five-to-seven percent of your brain that is active. Although you are unconsciously processing new information all the time, your mind organizes and categorizes how you conceptualize all new experiences based on similar situations that you have previously encountered. As an example, every time you see a red light when you are driving, you don't wonder, "What is that object doing in the middle of the road? What is that color? Is that a color? Is that red? Does that mean I should stop?" Instead, your foot automatically reaches for the brake pedal. Another common example is when the phone rings, you answer it.

When information comes in that doesn't make any sense, your mind scrambles to find any remotely similar circumstances that will help it make sense of the new information. If it is unable to find a way to categorize it, the information is either categorized incorrectly or disregarded as irrelevant. When your mind filters information in this way, you are missing out on a tremendous amount of significant information that would enable you to recognize the limitations that you currently operate within. We suggest that you consider updating your current filing system to include some new categories so that you are able to experience a new version of reality.

It is imperative for you to create some distance from yourself so that you can objectively observe the belief systems that you are basing your current perception of reality on. Begin to watch the choices that you make as if you were observing someone visiting a foreign country trying to figure out how to behave in an unfamiliar environment. Become aware of everything that you do as if you have never done it before. Brush your teeth with the other hand, make your bed upside down. Get out of any routine that you recognize you are in. There are some that you are not going to be able to recognize because they feel unavoidable, but if you do absolutely everything differently, it will shake you out of many of your habitual perceptions.

Are they saying to do everything differently because part of what is happening is that, as this new information comes in and we feel uncomfortable, our automatic response is to go back into familiar patterns? It is like a conditioned response?

Exactly. Although, keep in mind that conditioned responses and patterns are useful tools to engage in a third-dimensional version of reality. It is only as you desire to move beyond the third-dimensional experience that it becomes necessary to become more consciously aware of your experience. As you begin to consider this new perspective, we do not suggest that you no longer stop at red lights. We simply want to encourage you to begin to notice how habitual that and other behaviors are for you. Begin to notice how unconscious you are most of the time. The reason this is important is that, in order to be conscious, you need to recognize when you are not acknowledging information simply because it does not fit into your current perception of reality. This will become increasingly less difficult for you as the unused parts of your brain come online as you move further into the ascension process. The following meditation will help you assimilate these new ideas.

In this meditation, you are going to create a character representative of an issue or perspective that you feel strongly about. Then, you will create another character that represents an opposing point of view. Once you have created these two characters, you will imagine then fighting it out in a WWW Federation Wrestling arena. As an example, your character might be a warrior for peace and your opponent the United States government. As another example, your character might be someone who champions spirituality outside of traditional parameters and your rival a specific organized religion.

To begin, choose an issue that you want to focus on for this meditation. Now, imagine how that issue might be characterized as two opposing WWW Federation Wrestlers. Take a few minutes to think about the characteristics that each one might possess. Remember in the world of WWW Federation wrestling that everything is completely overdone, and each character is exaggerated to the point that it becomes a caricature. What are their genders? What do they look like? What are they wearing? What kinds of things might they say to each other? What kind of personality would each of them have? What would their names be? Ask yourself if this is the first time that you have been in the ring with them or if there is a history between the two of you. Are you friends? Are you enemies? Who comes into the ring with the upper hand?

Now, see the two of you go to the middle of the ring and

shake hands. Keep in mind that it is a fundamental element of WWW Federation Wrestling that the action is staged and set up beforehand, and that you are to follow a script for the benefit of the audience. Now, begin to play it out. You don't actually have to wrestle, although some of you will want the physicality of the wrestling. Perhaps you sit down to a game of chess, instead, or maybe you engage in a debate. The specifics of how the two of you play this out are unimportant. What matters is the illusion that you appear to be on opposite sides. You might even have prearranged signals like they have in baseball to cue each other. You can be as elaborate or as simple as you want to be for the purposes of this meditation.

Another key element in the world of WWW Federation Wrestling is that the match can appear to be going in the favor of one opponent—usually the one that overtly seems the most likely to win—then, unexpectedly, it will turn in favor of the underdog, who ends up winning.

This is the kind of situation that is literally going to play out in what you call reality in the next few years as the illusion of polarity crumbles. Doing this meditation a few times with the characters based on a variety of issues that you find difficult to deal with in your reality will allow you to become more adept at recognizing the illusionary nature of all that is around you. Have fun with this meditation, and then watch your world change...

The changes that are going to take place in the next ten years are going to be far greater than you understand at this point. Expect individuals, political organizations and global economic infrastructures to be unexpectedly and radically altered. As an example, imagine if the Catholic Church decided to put all of their money and resources into promoting information about moving the ascension process along. Just think about what would happen on a level of mass conscious awareness as a result of the dissemination of currently hidden information.

What should our roles be in terms of envisioning possible alternative realities, then? For example, should we envision the Catholic Church choosing to put all of their money and resources into teaching ancient scriptures?

It is merely a matter of considering the possibility. You don't have to hold the vision of what you want to manifest, merely consider it, and then let it go. What will happen as a result of doing this is that belief systems are going to be shaken loose on a mass consciousness level. That is why we gave such a physical exercise for the meditation. You might imagine that you have to be able to outmaneuver or out-visualize those who hold belief systems in opposition to yours. But the truth is that it only takes the conceptualization of a new possibility to have a domino effect on this entire illusionary reality.

The key here is that you don't have to figure out how to make it into reality; you simply have to conceive of the possibility. All that is yours to do is to consider as many possibilities as you can, and consequently, those possibilities have the potential to manifest as part of the mass consciousness version of reality. Eventually, as you become more conscious of experiencing yourself multidimensionally, you will be able to simultaneously experience all the possibilities that you envision playing out in your experience of reality.

It is a fundamental element of creation in a free-will zone such as this that you are never allowed to impose your version of reality onto anyone else. This means that, while you can envision an alternative reality for yourself, you must allow everyone else to create their own version of reality, as well. Each person on the planet at this time has the same creative potential that you do. They could not participate in this illusion of reality if they didn't. So, if they don't choose your version of reality, you need to remember that it is no big deal. It is merely another illusion!

What is the relationship between the multiple realities that we are constantly creating and the new possibilities for creation as mass consciousness shifts? Are they separate, or does the mass consciousness version of reality influence our creation?

They are interrelated, although it may be difficult to conceptualize. Consider how difficult it is to comprehend that you are simultaneously participating in parallel and multiple realities of your own creation at any given moment. When you exponentially expand that by taking into account that all of the Beings on the planet are also simultaneously creating their own versions of multiple perceptions of reality, you will have a sense of the extent of possible interpretations. A useful way to describe what you are experiencing now would be that each version of reality at this point is perceived as being mutually exclusive from all other versions. Right now, each Being buys completely into only one version of reality at a time, and they do not allow for the possibility of any other versions to impede on that reality. That will soon change, and realities are going to start bleeding into each other as the time/space concept that perpetuates the illusion of separation disappears.

These different versions of reality are not dependent on any other, and they are not necessarily interactive with one another. The best way to think about this is to recognize that you are creating multiple realities and that everyone around you is doing the same thing. Think about it holographically. Each conceptualized potential possibility changes all past and future possible perceptions of reality.

Then what happens when a group of people with like mind and spirit get together intentionally?

There is currently a great deal of misunderstanding about group consciousness. Consciously creating as a group fifth-dimensionally is much more potent than you can even imagine. At this time, when you come together in groups, it is more like a group mind than a gathering of individuals bringing different possibilities to the table. For the most part, you currently create as groups from a third-dimensional perspective using the intention-action-consequence formula. The reason that the group forms is the intention; what you do during meetings is the action; then, there are typically more meetings to discuss the consequences. Fifth-dimensional group creation, on the other hand, is beyond time/space, more organic, and closer to spontaneous combustion.

We don't mean to suggest that you not participate in groups. If you choose to be part of a group, you might find it useful to observe yourself as part of the group and as separate from the group, and also notice how the group defines itself in relation to those who are not included. Notice which thoughts you have that are in alignment with the thoughts of other group members and which thoughts you have that are different. You don't need to necessarily voice those thoughts that are different; just notice when you are less in sync with the group and/or when others seem to be deviating from the group norm. Notice your reaction and the reactions of other group members to differing perspectives. Recognize how embedded your current understanding of group is in the concept of polarity. A group is typically defined in terms of the shared goals or beliefs that are not shared by others outside of the group. Because it is based on the third-dimensional concept of duality, there is exclusivity inherent in the third-dimensional understanding of group.

Let's use the Catholic Church as an example. If we, as a group, were to go meet with a group of representatives from the Catholic Church to propose that they redistribute their resources, it is not likely that we would have any effect. Although, in reality, there is no separation between this group and the Catholic Church, from a third-dimensional perspective, we define ourselves as having opposing goals. It is our common feelings about how the Catholic Church uses their power that defines us as a group.

Another aspect of third-dimensional groups is that ideas are communicated with words, and that is a very slow, inefficient means of communicating. So much is lost when words are used. From a fifth-dimensional perspective, you would be unable to talk about what you are going to create as a group, because most of what is fueling the spontaneous combustion can't be verbalized. Begin to notice how strange it sounds to hear yourself speak. Notice how absurd words are. Notice how randomly things are named. We are not referring to any specific language. We are talking about the whole idea of how sounds are connected together to form words, many of which are quite random. Begin to notice which words actually resonate energetically with what you are referring to and which words don't. Once you begin to pay attention to this, you may hear or feel new words to define your reality, or you may simply lose interest in naming things and begin to rely more on how they feel to you.

If the time/space continuum is collapsing, does that mean that we will be able to see people from the past and future physically on

Earth?

Yes, you will be able to see people, as well as animals that have been considered extinct, such as dinosaurs.

Will only people that become conscious of the existence of multidimensional realties be able to see them, or will everyone see them?

As the time/space continuum collapses, you are going to realize that seemingly conflicting versions of reality operate all the time. Remember that each person creates their own version of reality and that all realities are illusionary. This means that there can be an infinite number of realities existing simultaneously. One aspect of becoming aware of multidimensional realities is that you begin to consciously recognize divergent realities and accept that they appear to be in contradiction with one another. It is commonly believed that if all realities were to converge, the world would become chaos. However, the truth is that it is impossible for them to converge, because each one exists independent of the others.

Part of this third-dimensional illusion is the belief on a collective consciousness level that chaos means the end of humanity as you know it. That is indeed what is happening, but from another perspective, it is the beginning of a new version of humanity as you become aware of yourselves from a multidimensional perspective. It takes the conscious awareness of realities converging to recognize that what you call reality is only an illusion. As you become increasingly aware of this happening, know that you have nothing to fear. Remember, you have set it up to happen this way. You are not in danger on any level.

I am struggling with honoring the choices of people who are making different choices than I am.

We understand that it seems paradoxical, but it really isn't. What we want you to understand is that it is time to make your choices about who you want to be, who you want in your life, and what you want to commit to. It is time to let go of those interactions with others that are holding you in the illusion of third-dimensional limitation. You must let go of any judgment you have about the choices that other people are making, even if they choose to continue to create their version of reality from a third-dimensional perspective. You cannot fully engage with your own creation of reality if you continue to focus so much of your attention on the creations of others. This is an opportunity for you to begin to recognize how your choices are creating your perception of reality and to understand that there are an infinite number of perceptions to choose from.

Do my choices have a different effect on future events than they do on past events?

There is no difference. It is only from a third-dimensional perspective that you perceive a difference between the past, present and future. Those concepts are only useful within the parameters of the illusion of time/space. Any time you make a choice, it affects your perception of reality throughout time/space. This means that it is as easy to change the past as it is to change the future. If you think about it, this is not a totally foreign concept. There are many examples of this in movies and books, such as the movie *Frequency* with Dennis Quaid, or *Terminator 2* with Arnold Schwarzenegger; the books by Madeleine L'Engle, like *A Wrinkle in Time,* or the *Chronicles of Narnia* by C.S. Lewis; and the television series *Star Trek*, especially *The Next Generation.*

You have talked about time. Is there anything that you want us to know about space?

Space and time are actually the same idea distinguished by different contexts. When you perceive it in terms of other time/space moments, you call it 'time.' When you perceive it in terms of physical manifestation, you call it 'space.' It may feel like a very advanced concept, but in fact, it is really very simple. Another way to conceptualize it is to think of space as visually perceptible and time as movement.

As you become more conscious that your choices determine your perception of reality, you will begin to recognize when you temporarily move beyond the illusion of time/space and then step back in again. You actually do this all the time now; it is just that you are so good at it that you don't recognize when you do it. What is going to change is that you are going to become consciously aware of doing it. For example, as you are having a particular experience, you might decide that you don't like how it is playing out, so you momentarily move out of time/space, make a different choice, and then step back into that same time/space moment, and it plays out differently than it would have otherwise.

We can give you an example of how this works from the television show *Buffy the Vampire Slayer.* Watching *Buffy* is another great way to expand your ideas about the limitations of time/space. In the first four seasons of the show, Buffy is an only child. Then, in the beginning of the fifth season, a sister shows up in the first episode. They don't explain it; Buffy just suddenly has a sister, Dawn. As it turns out, Dawn is actually a key that can be used to cause all realities to collapse in on each other, which everyone believes will cause the end of the world. Dawn has taken on human form to be protected by Buffy.

What is particularly interesting is that no one—including Buffy, her friends, even her mother—realizes that Dawn has not always been there. This is because when Dawn came into human form as Buffy's sister, each person who interacted with Dawn perceived a past with her that did not exist until the moment that she came into their lives. In other words, the past was changed to support the present illusion that Dawn was Buffy's sister. This is exactly what we are talking about.

As you begin to look beyond the illusion of time/space, you will be able to consciously alter your perception of reality at will. That is a significant step in becoming aware of the infinite multidimensional possibilities available to you in each moment. It is up to you to choose a different perspective, and you can do so only by recognizing the illusionary nature of the one that you now use to manifest your current version of reality.

Multidimensional Awareness

"Imagine entire universes existing into infinity within you."

How do we begin to conceptualize multidimensional awareness?

Imagine the concept of multidimensional awareness as an outline in the shape of a humanoid Being, and as you look through this human form, you are able to see universes and galaxies expanding into infinity. This would also be an accurate way to conceptualize the human manifestation of your energy. The point that we are trying to make is that there is no differentiation between the concept of multidimensional awareness and the concept of being human. It is merely a different focal point. In order to begin to comprehend the theory of multidimensional awareness, you must be willing to see beyond your limited perspective as conceptualized through your current third-dimensional understanding of what you call reality. We want each of you to imagine the outline of your body, and instead of the physicality that you are in the habit of recognizing, imagine entire universes existing into infinity within you, and keep this perspective of yourself in the back of your mind as we are talking throughout this session.

Would being consciously aware of multiple dimensions at the same time be analogous to being aware of our hand and our foot at the same time? In other words, being aware that two aspects of ourselves simultaneously co-exist in our awareness?

When you think about multidimensional awareness in terms of co-existence, there is an inherent assumption of separateness. In reality, there is no differentiation between dimensions. When we talk about the various dimensions as if they are separate and distinct from each other, we do so from a third-dimensional perspective. Each of you is already multidimensional. It is an innate aspect of being human to exist multidimensionally. It is merely the conscious awareness that you are multidimensional that is missing. When you begin to think about being multidimensional, the awareness that you exist multidimensionally immediately shuts down, because you can only define the concept of multidimensionality from a third-dimensional perspective. So, it is going to make it a little tricky to think and talk about multidimensionality in this session, but we are going to do it anyway!

In order to talk about multidimensional awareness, we need to dissect the concept. As we do this, it is important that you remember that we are using a third-dimension perspective. In reality, the different dimensions exist holographically. When anything exists as a holographic creation, each individual particle contains within it a complete cellular memory of the whole, and anything that affects the whole similarly affects each particle. Because humans are holographic, each cell in your body holds the cellular memory of your entire body and is affected equally. If you apply this concept to your understanding of dimensionality, the third dimension contains the cellular memory of absolutely everything from every other dimension; in turn, every other dimension contains the cellular memory of every aspect of the third dimension. Although it is useful to think about the different dimensions in terms of multidimensional awareness, always do so with the awareness that each dimension cannot exist without all of the others. It is not so much that they define each other as it is that they each offer a different perspective of the same experience. To get a feel for what we mean, you might envision that each dimension views reality through a different colored filter. For example, imagine that the third dimension lens is green, the fourth dimension might be silver, and the fifth dimension could be blue.

Is there is a unique structure that makes up each dimension?

Yes and no. Don't attach too literally to anything that we are saying.

There is not a structure exactly; it is not that rigid. The parameters of each dimension are more fluid than that, but you could say that each dimension is uniquely defined. Let the information that comes through during this session flow through you. Don't try too hard to figure it out with your mind. You will find that you have fleeting moments of great clarity, and in the next moment, the understanding will be completely lost. Allow the understanding to waft into and out of your awareness through all of your senses. Get a sense of the different dimensions through the colors that we have suggested by how they feel, instead of how you might imagine them to look.

As we become multidimensionally aware, how will that be different from our present awareness? What is it going to feel like?

The first difference you will notice is that you will have an increased awareness of what you are creating in each moment, automatically followed by you taking conscious responsibility for all of your creations. You are, of course, already creating all the time; however, at this point, you are surprised and caught off guard when what you have created manifests as part of your perceived reality. Once you become aware of your multidimensionality, you will no longer be able to pretend that you don't know what you are creating. Keep in mind that there is no judgment here, because the whole purpose of a third-dimensional illusionary reality is to enable you to experience your creation of reality as if it has been created by someone else, and engage with it as if it is happening *to* you.

As we said earlier, you are already multidimensional. What is shifting for you is the conscious awareness that you are. As you begin to become aware of the effect that you have on each person with whom you interact, and begin to recognize that your choices affect the whales in Australia as well as the growing season in Alaska, you will make very different choices. With every in-breath of possibility and every out-breath of creation, you will know the myriad ways that your choices affect absolutely everything. *That* is multidimensional awareness. Imagine breathing in, and as you breathe out, watching reality shimmer, shift and change before your eyes. That is, in reality, what already happens, despite the fact that you are not conscious that that is the case.

Is it only from a third-dimensional perspective that there is not an awareness of the other dimensions?

There is the potential and the possibility of multidimensional awareness in all dimensions. For example, in many dimensions there is an awareness of the third dimension, but it is not of any interest to them, so the awareness becomes irrelevant. In other dimensions, there is an intentional veil of forgetfulness around multidimensional awareness that is different than that which you have in place here. There are also dimensions in which the focus is to be aware of all the other dimensions for various reasons. Although the potential or the possibility for multidimensional awareness exists in all dimensions, the degree to which that awareness is conscious depends on what is being experienced in that dimension at any given time.

I'd like to know more about the fifth dimension. Can you give more specifics? For example, how is it different from the third dimension? How will we experience things differently? How do they communicate? What are their communities like?

The biggest difference between the third and fifth dimensions is that, in the fifth dimension, there is no distinction or separation from anyone or anything else, as you experience it third-dimensionally. Telepathy is the primary method of communication. Because time and space do not exist in the same way fifth-dimensionally, teleportation is a common way to move from one place to another. The term "community" would not be used fifth-dimensionally, because it is an integral part of fifth-dimensional existence, not a concept that is discussed. There is no dishonesty, no hidden agendas and no secrets. Power is understood differently. For example, how much power someone has is not defined in terms of the collective, and there is no correlation between power and sex. It is commonly understood that financial energy is infinite.

My understanding is that Earth is increasing her vibration and we have the opportunity to increase our vibration, as well, and that, by doing so, we will affect everything in the whole universe. Is that accurate?

Because all creation is holographic, when Earth increases her vibration, all life that exists within her energy field on all vibrational levels, as well as every particle throughout the universe, is affected. The same is true for any changes that you make within your vibrational field, because you also hold within each of your cells a memory of each particle throughout the universe—just as each of those particles holds the memory of each of your cells. Think back to the image that you envisioned at the beginning of this session of your human form as an outline containing infinite universes and galaxies. You are creating and altering entire universes with every breath.

One thing that is holding you back from becoming consciously aware of your multidimensionality is based on your concern that if you acknowledge your creations, you will have to maintain them or be responsible for them, and that seems like a lot of work to you. We want you to consider the possibility that, actually, the opposite is true. By becoming consciously aware of your creative potential and power in each out-breath, you will make things much easier on yourself. What happens now as you unconsciously create your reality is that you are continually surprised by what manifests, and it is as if you are continually putting out fires that you don't even realize you started. However, if you become more conscious about your creation, you will no longer be surprised by what manifests, and you will not set anything into motion that you would rather not have to deal with at a future time.

Another piece of this is that as you step back into conscious awareness of your multidimensionality, you will come face to face with your many lifetimes of unconscious creation. You resist doing this because you judge many of these creations to be catastrophes for which you will be held accountable. You currently carry in your cellular memory the incorrect idea that you have made mistakes. In reality, it is not possible for you to make a mistake. What is getting in your way is that you are interpreting what has happened solely through the filter of the third-dimensional perspective, and doing so does not allow you to see the whole picture. Once you are able to see your creations from beyond this limited point of view, you will be able to see the perfection in all that you have created.

How do we look at all this drama and trauma as if nothing was a mistake?

A good place to begin is to recognize that everyone who participated in each of these experiences did so by choice. Because you currently exist in a free-will zone, it can be no other way. Another useful perspective is to remember that you cannot destroy anyone or anything. Everything and everyone that exists in your reality is made up of energy, and it is a universal law that energy cannot be destroyed; it can only change form.

What has happened is that how you felt when you participated in these experiences has frozen within your energy field, and your memory of those experiences is now filtered through your isolated emotional perception. As a result, you also believe that everyone else who participated in those same experiences remembers it from the same perspective that you do. In reality, they remember it entirely differently and do not blame you.

Let's use the atom bomb as an example. The atom bomb in and of itself was just another way to use energy. When the concept of atomic energy was initially conceived, it had nothing to do with being used as a weapon of destruction. There was great excitement in the early days of experimenting with atomic energy about the possibilities and potential of being able to control and utilize such a massive amount of energy. You have to understand that each individual who participated in the early days of exploring atomic energy chose not to be consciously aware of the potential of it being used to destroy humanity. It was also the choice of each individual who was eventually affected by the destruction caused by the atomic bomb to experience atomic energy from that perspective.

You have the mistaken belief, based on these frozen memories that you hold within your cellular memory, that your choices and actions have taken something away from others against their will. That is not possible. Any experience that you might currently interpret as destructive was simply an opportunity for many Beings to change form. It is of utmost importance that you recognize each individual's choice to participate in these experiences and that you know that no one, at any time, has been destroyed. They simply changed form. You need to remember that no one is perpetually trapped in that moment of terror and death where you imagine them to be. It is only your interpretation of the experience, based on the frozen memory that you are using to define what happened, that makes it seem that way. You must allow energy to move that frozen memory into present time, and recognize that everyone has moved on to other experiences.

It is when aspects of your cellular memory become frozen in the past that your multidimensional awareness shuts down. It is only when you deny the perfection of all that you create that it is possible to have judgment about any manifestation of reality. When you first conceived the idea of participating in this whole third-dimensional planetary experience, it was quite fascinating to you. As you were considering the infinite experiences that you could have before you moved your consciousness into this manifestation of reality, you couldn't conceive of what it would be like to experience yourself as separate from everyone else. And when it actually happened, you went into shock, and you now have all these fragmented, frozen pieces in your energy field. It was, at the time, the most effective way for you to be able to continue to participate in this version of reality.

It can be compared to going on a roller coaster. At first, you watch the people already on it. You hear them screaming, and you think that sounds like fun. Then you go on it yourself, and when you get to the top and are about to plummet down, you realize that it is much higher than it looked from the ground, but at that point you can't do anything about it, and down you go. That is similar to what you have experienced throughout this manifestation of reality. You need to understand that you are fully committed to playing this experience out, regardless of what happens, and that you have done what you had to do to stay in it.

We like the analogy of the roller coaster because it is a choice that you make, not something that is imposed upon you. The distinction here is between the ideas of responsibility and ownership. Ownership is active, and involves conscious awareness of the fact that you are creating your experience. Responsibility is reactive, and involves trying to keep everything on track from the perspective that you have no control over what is happening to you. One aspect of becoming more multidimensionally aware is that you begin to become conscious of your creative power.

Another aspect of becoming more multidimensionally aware is

that you experience everything as happening much more quickly. When we do the meditation, you will get of sense of how that feels like. Moving out of the illusion of density and into multidimensional awareness means moving into lightness, fun, love, and conscious creation. You don't have time to process everything third-dimensionally right now. That would take months, and there are much more interesting things to do with that time. You are done with processing. You are ready to quantum leap into lightness, and you are going to make great strides in that direction tonight.

Have we come from higher dimensions or other dimensions?

You are simultaneously operating in higher dimensions. You have never been separate; you have just believed that you were.

During dreamtime, can we travel to those other dimensions where we also operate?

Yes, you can. That awareness is also starting to seep into your daily life. Perhaps you will hear just a bit of a melody, or you will hear something on the wind or from distant chimes. You might smell an unexpected scent, or feel an emotion waft through that is unrelated to what is happening for you in that moment. You could sense someone attempting to communicate with you on the very edge of your mind. Many of you here tonight know what we are talking about and are very excited about what is coming next. You would not be hearing these words if it was not time for you to take the next step. This means something different for each person here, but it is, without exception, a quantum leap in conscious awareness of your multidimensionality for each one of you.

How can we become conscious of what we are creating multidimensionally?

The conscious part is not going to be as difficult as you think. You keep almost doing it, but your mind isn't recognizing that you are doing it. The most useful thing you can do is to stop thinking about becoming multidimensionally aware, and behave, instead, as if you already possess that awareness. Everything that you are looking for is already right in front of you and all around you. You simply need to choose to begin to perceive your reality from a multidimensional perspective in addition to a third-dimensional perspective. Notice that we say in addition to, not instead of. With but a slight shift in perspective, each of you can easily do this. You know that feeling just as you are falling asleep? When you know you are not awake, but you are not really asleep? It is at that moment that you are essentially between dimensional realities. As you go about your day, strive to recall that feeling. You have to *feel* it, not *do* it.

Is it a matter of shifting where you place your attention or changing your focus?

Not exactly, because thinking in terms of attention or focus is still *doing*. You simply need to recall what it feels like. To return to the going-to-sleep analogy, sometimes just as you begin to fully relax, you have a muscle spasm that jars you back into full consciousness, and you momentarily wake up again. That is what is happening right now on the feeling level. When you get close to that feeling of moving back into awareness of your multidimensionality, you choose to move back into the illusion that you are only third-dimensional.

As the veil thins, individual and group realities will begin to separate out from the mass consciousness version of reality and become optional alternative versions of reality. Until now, most humans have experienced their creation of a third-dimensional illusion of reality at some point along the continuum of the mass consciousness version of reality, with one end of the continuum being to unconsciously participate in the idea that reality is created for them, and the other end of the continuum being to explore the possibility that they are creating their reality. When individuals and groups begin engaging with their experience of reality beyond this continuum, new paradigms are created. As individuals and groups create new possibilities, they are, in effect, designing new templates that others can use for future creations of reality.

Another aspect of the thinning of the veil is that the differentiation between individual versions of reality will become less defined, and as a result, it will become increasingly difficult for many people to distinguish their creation from the creation of others. This is why it is vital that you become conscious of what you are creating, and learn to recognize when you are unconsciously participating in someone else's creation.

When Beings engage with their reality as if it is created for them, they often unconsciously participate with whatever version of reality seems most exciting, and this is often a version that involves a lot of drama and fear. The manifestation of war is a perfect example of this. It didn't take much to perpetuate the illusion that our current war was inevitable. It was like dropping a match in an extremely dry forest. In this analogy, the forest symbolizes the many Beings who choose to believe that their reality is created for them.

As you begin to become conscious of multidimensional possibilities, it may seem as if there is so much sensory input that you find it difficult to ascertain what is your creation and what is the creation of others. A good place to start would be to notice when your emotion changes. Notice when you suddenly feel different than you did a moment before. You might feel uncomfortable or sad or angry or even happy or excited. It is important to remember that emotions are always information, and it would be useful to ask your guidance, "Is this my creation?" or "Does this have anything to do with me?" Know that you will always get an immediate and accurate answer.

If it is yours, the next question to ask is, "What does this mean?" Then, listen for the answer. Don't ask, "What can I do about this?" because that immediately puts you back into doing. You may need to practice asking questions and receiving answers from your guidance. Remember, the answers that you receive may come to you in the form of sensing, knowing, smelling, feeling, hearing, tasting or seeing, and may even be beyond the six senses. You might get the answer in the form of color or music or geometrical shapes, or numbers or a combination of any or all of the above—or something you can't even define. You might even receive another emotion.

One way of denying your multidimensional awareness is when you ask a question and wonder why you don't get an answer. You always get an answer, but if it doesn't make sense to you within the context of your cognitive awareness, you usually disregard it or change it. So if you get an answer that doesn't make sense, keep asking questions until it does make sense. Be open to new and unexpected ways that the answers might come to you. Begin to recognize that part of becoming multidimensionally aware is to expect answers, and if they are not immediately evident, to ask again in a different way, instead of assuming that you were not answered.

Here is a practical way to do this: at any point during the day, you can simply ask, "What sensory information am I missing right now?" In any given moment, there is always more going on than what you are aware of from a third-dimensional perspective. It is a good idea to do this when nothing unusual seems to be happening so that you can get in the habit of doing it. Practicing this will help you begin to distinguish that there is more than one version of reality available in any moment.

At first, you will find that you are able to conceptualize two versions at once, and then three or four, and eventually, many more than that. It is important to understand that multiple versions of reality often appear to contradict one another, so don't automatically discount information that you receive if things don't seem to fit together. Each version of reality is independent of all other versions; therefore, there is no reason why they should make sense within the context of each other. Because so much is happening in every second, it will never be boring. You are going to have so much fun with this new awareness! You are going to be delighted at how much more there is to experience!

You know how much fun babies and small children have laughing and giggling at what appears to be nothing? If you watch them, they seem to see things that aren't there. Animals also do this when they seem to see or hear things that you don't. Children and animals are great examples of being aware of simultaneous versions of reality. All of you had this awareness as small children, so the idea is not entirely foreign to you. We suggest that you spend some time with young children and animals, and try to see what they see.

Dick Cheney is saying that there is definitely going to be another terrorist attack. To me, sending that kind of information out to the whole nation means that if enough people believe it, they will create it.

They are not intentionally trying to set that reality into motion. It is because they believe another attack to be inevitable that they are trying to convince the world that they have some control over the situation, despite the fact that they know they don't. That is a good example of unconscious creation of reality.

I'm not sure I believe that they are not aware of what they are creating.

Some Beings who work for the government are aware of the influence of propaganda, but most of them aren't aware of their own creative power, or of others'. Most government officials don't want these things to happen any more than you do. What you see on television are actions taken based on fear. They truly do intend it to be a warning and do not realize that it will manifest if enough people choose it as reality.

We are not saying that there are not Beings in the government who intentionally manipulate the public, but you need to remember that the government is made up of individual Beings who are each creating their own version of reality, or choosing to participate in the government version of reality. You need to remember that these are people with families who own property and are attached to the lives that they have created. At the same time, because they choose to work for the government, they are also part of a group that perpetuates particular versions of reality. It is important to understand that there are different echelons of the government, and at the highest levels, yes, there are those who are aware of manipulating mass consciousness on this creative level, and on other levels, there are those who are consciously manipulating public opinion for particular agendas.

However, most Beings who work for the government do so from a perspective where they honestly believe that they are doing what is best for the American people. While it is true that they are perpetuating versions of reality that are being consciously generated by those in higher echelons of the government, they remain unconscious of the fact that they are doing so. Remember, it ultimately comes down to each individual's choice of which version of reality they choose to participate in, and the government-generated version is only one of a multitude of choices. While it may be tempting to think of the government as a single unit trying to manipulate you, that is a very third-dimensional perspective of "us" against "them." It is another possibility to consider the government as a group made up of a multitude of Beings, each choosing which version of reality they want to participate in.

I don't choose to create another war, so I don't choose to believe that it is inevitable.

When you think solely in terms of having a war or not having a war, you are still participating along the continuum of the mass consciousness version of reality. Choosing to move away from war or choosing to move towards war is still accepting war as a possible version of reality. If you choose instead to move onto a different continuum entirely, you can begin to create new templates of reality that do not involve war one way or another. Another common approach is to surround those Beings who support the war in light and love with the intention that they will see the error of their ways. We don't suggest that you do that, because the underlying assumption is that your version of the mass consciousness version of reality is more valid than theirs. Regardless of where you choose to participate on the continuum of the mass consciousness version of reality—even if you are opposed to it—you are still perpetuating its existence.

In the following meditation, we are going to give you the opportunity to free up those places in your energy field where your energy has been frozen.

To begin this meditation, we want you to imagine what it feels like when you know that you have set something into motion that will inevitably come back to haunt you. You may not know exactly how it is going to play out, but you do know that it is not going to be pleasant, and you feel as if you have no control over what is going to happen. The details are not important; simply recall the feeling. This is how those frozen parts of your energetic field are experienced. It is as if you are perpetually "waiting for the other shoe to drop" on an unconscious level, and it is affecting all aspects of your current experience of reality.

Now, we are going to remind you of some historical events, the experiences of which many of you have stored inaccurately in your cellular memory. We want you to notice what you feel as we name them, and when you begin to feel a sense of trepidation, focus on that feeling. Again, do not focus on the details of the experience if they begin to come back to you; only focus on the feeling. Okay, here we go: the end of Lemuria; the destruction of Atlantis; the Great Flood; the Ice Ages; Egypt; the Crusades; the Dark Ages; The World Wars; the Holocaust; the Salem witch hunts, the genocide of any race in human history that you are aware of. Now, focus on that feeling, and imagine that it looks and feels like a piece of coal. It is dense and dark and heavy...

Now, imagine that this piece of coal contains the memory of your experience of whatever triggered the feeling of trepidation for you. Know that the coal contains the entire experience, and feel it getting increasingly dense. Feel the density momentarily, and then watch as it suddenly shatters into a million pieces, and watch as all these pieces float gently out into space. Feel the release. Feel the relief. As all of those pieces of coal move out of your energy field, recognize that your memory of that experience had been frozen into a dense, dark holding pattern that has been affecting each and every version of reality that you have created since that time. Know without a doubt that you have now freed that energy to be used to create new templates of reality. As each particle flies away, recognize that it possesses its own consciousness. Know that each particle of energy came to you to assist you in creating the version of reality that you are now dissolving, and allow it to return to the realm of creation with your gratefulness and your blessing.

Now, return your awareness to the place in your energetic field where that feeling had been stored for so long, and notice how different it feels now. Feel the movement, potential and possibility where that dense, dark accumulation of energy used to be. You might see it beginning to grow and evolve into something new right before your eyes. You have moved back into creation, back into the perpetual, limitless opportunity to experience yourself in a multitude of ways that is creation. Know that releasing this density within your cellular memory has a holographic effect all over your energy field, and what you have released exponentially opens up multitudes of new ways to experience who you are throughout time.

Expect new ideas and new possibilities to come to you in the days, weeks and months ahead. See new sprouts beginning all over your energetic field. You have changed everything. These are all the ideas that you have been feeling at the edge of your mind, or have been beginning to think about, but have not been quite sure where to go with them. They are all sprouting like crazy. You are going to be full of new ideas, and they are going to come to you in ways they never have before because of doing this meditation. Notice how light and expansive you feel. Notice how hopeful you feel.

See the outline of the shape that you know yourself to be as human, and now look into that form to see the infinity that you are. Imagine that you walk around the back of that form, and when you look back, you see planets and galaxies and universes. Now, walk around to the front of that form, and see another whole kind of infinity. Remember, this is who you are. Recognize the creative potential that you have available to you at all times. See all the new sprouts throughout your energy field that used to be dense spots. You have freed up such a tremendous amount of energy. Take a moment now to feel the difference. Know that, with this new awareness and expansiveness, you now offer a new template for creating reality.

Know that this meditation is not one that you will need to do again. It is complete. As you feel ready, bring your awareness back to this room, and slowly open your eyes.

☸

Who has been speaking to us through the Records for this session?

We have been speaking from a collection of experience from the past, present and future in relation to multidimensional awareness. As humans, you imagine yourselves to be concrete and third-dimensional, but your sense of who you are is, in reality, a composite of your experiences throughout time. You are not nearly as definitive as your minds imagine you to be. We would suggest that, in addition to asking who is answering your questions about multidimensional awareness, you also recognize who is asking for information. You will realize that it is each of you, in your limitless multidimensional understanding, who is both asking and answering the questions presented here tonight.

Remember at the beginning of the session, when we asked you to imagine a Being called "Multidimensional Awareness?" You imagined yourself as human, and you imagined multidimensional awareness as this immense, expansive concept. Now you realize that there is, in reality, no differentiation between the two. They are merely two different expressions of the same energy. The importance of the outline of the human form that we keep referring to is simply a symbolic representation of the parameters within which you are creating your current versions of reality. Becoming more aware of how you are operating third-dimensionally inevitably leads to the conscious awareness of how multidimensional you actually already are.

Ascension

"When you are creating your reality from an ascended state, you can pick up a much wider range of frequencies."

Can you define ascension?

We define ascension as increasing the amount of light and the speed of the vibration in your energy field, which, in turn, allows you to pick up frequencies beyond the third dimension and to become aware of the multidimensional aspects of yourself.

What do we have to do to ascend?

All you have to do is set the intention that you want to ascend, and that intention sets the process into motion. If you are interested in the concept of ascension, you have already set the intention. Once you set the intention, the next step is to become aware that you are in the ascension process.

What will the physical changes be throughout the ascension process?

As an exercise for your mind, we want you to try to phrase your questions as if ascension has already taken place. It is not something into which you are moving; it is not something that is going to come. It has already happened. You just have not recognized that it has already happened. Think about it in terms of being an observer of something that has already occurred, as opposed to being a participant in a future event, and this will help you to recognize that it has already taken place for you.

Can you explain the significance of the physical things that we are experiencing as we become ascended Beings?

You are already noticing them. These are the things that we have been talking about in these sessions. Remember, the semantics are a little tricky, because everything happens at once, and that means that everything we are talking about has already happened. We have been talking about ascension the entire time that we have been doing this series of readings. Some of the physical symptoms that are part of the ascension process we have discussed are the tiredness, the increased synchronicity in your life, the increased emotion that you feel, the increased frustration, and the putting on of weight.

Notice that putting on weight looks like the opposite of ascension, because you are getting heavier instead of lighter, but remember, we have also talked about the key to ascension being complete descension onto the planet. So, experiencing all of these things we have been talking about are just indications that you are more fully moving into being on the planet. You are sleeping more prior to moving into the ascension process because you were not as grounded as you thought you were. We can interchangeably use the idea of being grounded and descension, because they are the same thing.

Remember, being grounded does not mean shutting down your awareness of higher information. Being grounded refers to being strongly rooted in the Earth while that information is coming in, so you can be a conduit and allow information to easily move in and out of your energy field. Being descended means remembering who you are beyond the third dimension while participating in this third-dimensional illusion of reality. Once you are more consciously in physicality, you will require more sleep so that you will be able to participate more consciously while you are awake.

When you are creating your reality from an ascended state, you can pick up a much wider range of frequencies, much like dogs can hear sounds that humans cannot hear, elephants can communicate with each other over exceptionally far distances, and whales and dolphins can communicate with radar. These are some of the abilities that you are going to become aware of in yourself. As you become more conscious of these abilities, you will be presented with new possibilities for creating your reality. This is why we have talked in earlier sessions about the importance of becoming aware of the fact that you are recreating the illusion of physicality in every moment.

As you have moved into ascension, you have also moved more fully into your body. Because of that, it is now more observable when you leave your body. You feel tired and you sleep more. When you have emotions, you feel them more strongly than you do when you are ungrounded, because you are more physically in your body. Experiencing feelings is part of the physical experience. It might seem contradictory, but the more you move into your body, the more you will become consciously aware of your multidimensional experiences.

So, the contrast is more evident?

Yes. Before, you were not quite here and you were not quite there, so moving in-between was not as noticeable. Consequently, the more you are consciously here, the more noticeable it becomes when you are not here. This ties in with the other things we have talked about concerning the conscious creation of reality. In an earlier session, we said that you needed to become aware of where you were, when you were, and what was happening when you were in different places, in different states, and interacting in different ways. Those were the beginning steps, and now, you can consciously compute all of those aspects of your reality simultaneously.

It may not seem like a big deal, but it is huge for you to be consciously aware of your physicality in this time of transition. Conscious ascension has not been done before in this way, and it is not something that you are going to do in the future, because you are already in the middle of doing it. We are in awe of you, because you have not exploded. You have not gone crazy. You are all functioning increasingly well throughout this process. No one expected it to go this well. We don't mean to imply that you were set up like rats in a lab. You knew that if the plan went wrong, you would return to source, or simply ascend sooner, so the worst-case scenario was not unbearable. Remember, too, that you orchestrated this plan together with us. You were the braver ones. We were the ones that said, "Let's see how it goes for them, and we will try it next time." You said, "I want to do it now; I don't care if I blow up," and jumped right in to the experience with both feet.

What is it going to feel like, or how are we going to feel differently, when we have completed the ascension process?

For starters, you are going to stop thinking about it and talking about it so much. Basically, when you don't care anymore, you will know that the ascension process has been completed. It will no longer be something that you are striving for or thinking about continually. When you are there, you are going to be interested in other things. This is a very relevant question, because presently, you are all focusing so hard on the idea of ascension being something in the future or something outside of yourself that you cannot see that you are ascended. Every time you say, "When am I going to ascend?" all of your guides say, "You are ascended." Then, you say, "When am I going to ascend? Why don't you answer my question?" and your guides repeat, "You are ascended." Then, you get frustrated and demand, "Well, when am I going to ascend?" This is what you do continually, and we think it is humorous. However, since you find it frustrating, we will not laugh at you. In fact, even though you cannot see it, you have already accomplished ascension.

That is why we prefaced this reading with the importance of changing your perception. Ascension is not something that you need to do; it is not a state to be achieved. In fact, it is no different than where you are already. This is heaven on Earth. You are heaven on Earth. Do not be confused by the fact that there are wars going on around Earth. This is heaven on Earth. Heaven is a perception of reality, and you contain heaven. You are the molecules that establish the presence of heaven in this time/space moment, and to take it a step further, you always have been. Ascension is just a more conscious awareness of the heaven that you are at any given moment. Even though we are teasing you about how you think about ascension and continue to ask so much about it, we know you need that intellectual interest to propel your consciousness in that direction. It can be compared to the power that fuels a spaceship or a rocket ship into space. The questioning and the asking to understand ascension is what has enabled you to get to where you are now.

Keep in mind that much of what has happened is beyond your consciousness. The questioning has been an interesting way to keep your consciousness otherwise occupied while the rest of your energy field went on with the process. As we have said in other sessions, it was useful to do things to entertain your mind and to keep your mind busy. Thinking and talking about ascension has kept your mind quite occupied. Good job! We are going to say the word now, and we want you to feel it. Do not hear it. Do not think about it. Do not listen to it. Just feel it. *Ascension...* See? That is all it is. Now, we can go back to talking about it, if you want to.

As we gain awareness of the other dimensions and alternative realities, will we be able to move from one to the other, and back to the third dimension? Is that what we are planning to do?

Yes, and you are already doing that. The part you are going to change is that you are going to begin noticing what you are doing. The awareness is already there; it is peeking through. Let's give you some examples of how you have experienced this without recognizing it. One way to know this is happening is to recognize that decisions have become easier for you. Have you noticed this yet? There was a point when making decisions was excruciating for you. There were so many options that you felt that any time you made a decision, you were leaving so much behind, or that everything was riding on each and every choice, even small ones. Remember how overwhelming that felt a few months ago? Now, it is not like that. Now, you just make decisions, one after another. That is an example of tuning in to multidimensional awareness. You can see how you are not really choosing; you are merely focusing. That, in and of itself, makes the act of making decisions much easier.

I need clarification on that. Is it like the feeling we have when we make the decision to simply let go, and allow the choice that we made to come into fruition? that moment of, "Okay, I am just going to choose. This feels right in the moment," and then trust?

Yes. You say that as if it is no big deal to reach that feeling. Two months ago, that feeling was very difficult for you to achieve. You could not find the peace in making decisions. That feeling makes such logical sense to your mind and seems like a common experience now, but recognize that it is very different than it was a couple of months ago. The deciding is still mental, and as soon as you make the decision and say, "I wonder what is going to happen," that split second is it, because it is at that moment that you have let go of control and just put it out there. It is that moment when it is out of your hands that you have become more comfortable with. Well done!

That feeling is very similar to the feeling you experience just as you surrender to sleep. Focusing on that feeling is a useful way to get used to the ascension process that you are experiencing. It is not concrete. It is very nebulous and in continuous movement. That is very similar to what being consciously aware of your ascension feels like. All the details that occupy your waking life, all the decisions, all the choices, all the options, are distracting you from your awareness of ascension—but remember that you have set them in place prior to now so you would be able to keep a foot in both worlds. We suggest you try being in that undecided place more often, because that is going to be good practice for moving between the third and fifth dimensions.

Just for the record, you are ahead of schedule. You were a bit behind for a while, and now you have moved ahead of schedule, which is really playing havoc with timelines and the third-dimensional concept of time/space. You might notice that things that have been predicted are happening sooner; this is happening in personal readings, as well. Events that were supposed to be a year or a year-and-a-half down the road are happening now.

So, behave as if the future that you have been working towards is here now. When you are presented with a decision that involves financial energy, make your choice as if you have all the money you need to do what is yours to do, because you do. In relationships, behave as if the person with whom you want to have a relationship already has all the awareness you have; the relationship will either fall apart or come together more quickly. Behave as if you are a Divine Master walking on Earth, because indeed you are. Behave as if you are Jesus walking on Earth. That is the closest example of a Divine Master that we can give you of whom you would be aware—

and he only knew a tiny part of what you know. Think about the miracles that he performed, and know they are within your power. We are talking about alchemy, manifesting reality, changing the weather, et cetera.

When I think about war going on in the Middle East, I don't resonate with that, or that is not my reality. In effect, that is a different reality. Is that correct?

Yes. Imagine that the thought forms that create war are within you, instead of outside of you. Place those Beings who are experimenting with the thought forms that create war within your heart, and let them play it out. By doing that, you can keep it from affecting other thought forms that you are engaging with as you create your current reality. Rather than holding the thought forms at arm's length and not having the war be part of you, put them inside of you. Put those Beings participating in that reality into your very heart, in a safe, loving place, and let them play out their version of reality. It can be compared to a child having a tantrum. When a child is throwing a tantrum, from the child's perspective, he or she has a valid reason for being upset. The child just need a safe place to work it out, so you make it safe for him or her to do that. Think about it in that way.

What if a person does not put any energy towards thinking about what is going on anywhere else? What does that mean?

It just means that it is of no interest to you. As we have said before, if it is interesting to you pursue it; if it isn't, don't. Let's take it to another level. If you do not think about it, it simply plays out differently than if you were to think about it. It is not better or worse. The behavior that is least useful in this scenario is worrying about it, or trying to save or help the people involved, or attempting to change what is happening. That is merely you asserting your perception of reality onto another's perception of reality with the assumption that your perception is better. By you simply choosing to not pay any attention to it whatsoever, it is allowed to flourish and become what it is meant to be. War is present on Earth at this time, in part, to balance the increasing light. Notice that as the light energy increases on the planet, the dark energy increases, as well. As you are becoming more enlightened, the war is also intensifying. There is a direct connection there. This is an experience of polarity, and it must be that way for a time.

How can we become more aware of being in the less dense fifth-dimensional vibration? I have a picture in my mind, as a result of some of the other readings, that we will be transitioning into a physical form or a lack of physical form that is different from this one. If we are already ascended, then I am assuming we are coexisting, or sort of flipping back and forth, between realities. How do we lessen the separation, and bring back the memory or the understanding of being in that less dense space?

The most useful thing you can do is to go back to the exercises and meditations that we have given you in earlier sessions. The primary thing that is getting in your way is your memory of when this has played out differently. When you have become close to this point in other lifetimes, you have suffered because of it. You have been tortured or killed or have destroyed others. It is that cellular memory that is keeping you from remembering now. It is your mind's way of protecting you. It can be compared to when something really traumatic happens to someone that causes him or her to block it out because of their inability to cope with the memory. That is what you have done. You have blocked out the memory of who you are beyond your third-dimensional expression, because from your mind's perspective, it has not ended well in the past. All of you have reached this place of awareness before in places like Egypt, Peru or Tibet. Then, as soon as you remembered, you either ascended immediately, or the armies broke the door down and your physical body was hurt, or others were destroyed because of your knowledge.

As soon as you remember who you are and regain access to your cellular memory, you will remember absolutely everything you have experienced, and you will no longer be able to operate under the illusion of separation. When you reached that point in the past, if you had not made peace with all of your choices and actions that were encoded in your cellular memory, your mind could not bear it, and you went insane. Remember the meditation from the *Multidimensional Awareness* session that helped you to release the stuck, dark places within you, allowing the energy to disperse and return to where it originated? The purpose of that meditation was to help you remember that everything that you have done, and everything that has been done to you, was allowed only through the agreement of everyone involved. It is important that the energy you have been holding within your cellular memory is now released so it does not continue to support the illusion of separation.

As we have suggested in earlier sessions, begin to appreciate and understand the role of your emotions on a day-to-day basis. Stop being afraid of them. Stop being afraid of those dark parts within you. You know that there are dark places within you, and because you do not acknowledge those parts of yourselves, you imagine that much more of you is dark than actually is in reality. If you were to look, there are only tiny pieces of darkness left, so go ahead and look. See what is really there. Recognize how much of you is light. Then, imagine the light enveloping the few remaining dark, shadowy places. Know that the dark places within you to which we refer are not even dense and dark at this point—they are just shadowy.

You are in the habit of seeing yourself in your third-dimensional expression. Begin to recognize that you can begin to see who you truly are and to show others who you truly are. There are not going to be any painful repercussions this time around. That is what is new and exciting about this particular time/space moment. Your mind may say, "I am not going there again. I did it fifteen times already, and each time, it turned out badly. I know what this looks like." However, the truth is that you do not know what is going to happen. This is a new experience. We are going to do a meditation later on to further assist you with this concept, but just know that the biggest thing getting in your way of remembering who you are is the idea that you are not worthy because of the remaining darkness within your energy fields.

In earlier readings, the Records indicated that we were going to ascend in waves, and that large groups of Beings were going to ascend together. Is that still the plan? Is that still what is going to happen?

Yes, that is still the plan. Initially, there are going to be small groups. Then, the groups are going to get increasingly larger; eventually, the groups will be made up of entire races of Beings. Toward the end of the ascension process, thousands and hundreds of thousands and millions of Beings will ascend together. The process will progress much more quickly as the groups get larger, but in the beginning, it will take more time, with smaller groups comprised of a few hundred or a few thousand Beings.

The Beings in this room are going to go individually or in small groups. The initial groups will be made up of twelve to thirty-six people. You are not the first wave; you are part of the second or third wave, although it is hard to talk about it linearly. Many Beings who have already ascended have worked out some of the kinks, but there is still much to be worked out, since this kind of mass ascension is unprecedented.

One of the reasons ascension is not yet happening in large groups is that, by participating in a group experience, an individual's experience is magnified exponentially. Any mental resistance or physical discomfort is greater when Beings are working together in groups. Your job is to work through this process. You are going through it very slowly, at first, in order to look at all the fear and the angst and the anxiety that you are feeling, frame by frame, to see what can be done differently to make the process more comfortable for Beings in future ascension waves. That is part of why it is so important for you to pay attention to your emotions and to become more conscious about your experience. You are creating the template for future ascension.

We are editing the film?

That is a great way of looking at it! When you are editing a film, it is comprised of action that has already taken place. Ascension has already happened. Now, you are going back and looking at the film frame-by-frame and saying, "Oh look, I was doing fine, and then I just wigged out here. What exactly happened in this frame that caused me to suddenly lose all of my trust and all of my faith? Was it something that happened on a mass consciousness level? Was it something that came up from my cellular memory?" You ask questions like that, and the information is uploaded to a place where all the ascension experience is being compiled. Then, the process is changed to make it easier and sent back to humanity through channels like this.

Remember how we used the analogy of the acts of a play in *The Human Experience* session? Part of you continues to play out the first act, and the part of you that is in Act Four sends information back to the part of you that is performing the first act over and over again. That information, in turn, causes you to change how you perform Act One each time. Much like that, the ascension process is being replayed over and over again in order to work out the kinks and to make it as effortless as possible for future groups of Beings. The movie *Groundhog Day* with Bill Murray is a humorous depiction of this idea.

What can you tell us about this group?

Each of you here is from a different soul group and comes from different lineages or different combinations of lineages. As a group, you can play out many different variables, both individually and collectively, and your experience is synthesized into something that can be brought back to other groups. There are other groups of Beings doing the same thing. There are also Beings who are not here today who are part of this group and have participated at different points. Some of them are not here today because they have taken the understandings gained from other readings out into the world in order to gather information to bring back to future readings. Some of you have also been doing that, and that is why you have not been here for every session.

This process of energy exchange is happening all the time. Just imagine how much energy has been pulled out of this Earth experience and then brought back in to change subsequent experience. The collected experiences are recorded in the Akasha and are reconciled with what is already known. At this point, knowledge about the ascension process is becoming highly refined. The ascension energy was initially very rough, and now it is becoming quite polished. You have already worked out much of the discomfort through your third-dimensional experiences. You are held in great honor, and we are in awe of how much you have run through your physical bodies. The fact that you have any remaining physical bodies after what you have been through is pretty awe-inspiring! Let that be another way you know that you have ascended. You could not have put your bodies through those experiences without having already moved into the ascension process. Your bodies could not have handled it.

And your minds...oh, we want to talk about your minds! They are doing so well. They keep expanding and expanding, and when you think they cannot expand any more and you give yourself permission to rest, they expand even more. You have done so well! You have followed the suggestions that we have made, and you have allowed yourselves to evolve in quantum leaps and bounds. You are so special. You are going to go down in the ascension history books as the original creators of Ascension 101. The hard part is over. It is much smoother sailing from here. You are going to still have some struggles within your mind, but overall, it is as if you have been on a bumpy road, and the paved part is now before you.

When you talk about us moving through the ascension process, my concern is that maybe things are going to happen before I am ready, that there will be all of this new knowledge all of a sudden, and I will not know what to do with it. Are you saying that everyone is moving along at his or her own pace? If we are part of a group that is going to go through the final process together, are we going to be waiting for those people? Or are we going to move back and forth? How is that all going to work?

This gets into the multidimensional aspects of group. We have talked in other sessions about some of the problems that third-dimensional groups encounter. Consider the possibility that everyone in a particular group does not have to move along the same time line. Let's say that there are ten people in a group; three of those people remember who they are beyond their third-dimensional expressions and, consequently, ascend. Then, because it was so fun, they come back and do it again, and right before they do it the second time, they tell a couple of other people in the group about their experience. This time, two more members of the group ascend with them. Then, those five people are so thrilled by the experience that they come back to do it yet again, and this time, they tell everyone else in the group. Then, the third time, the entire group ascends together.

Although it might appear that it happened over three phases, in actuality, the same moment is being replayed over and over again in a different way. It is not that anyone is ahead or that anyone is being left behind. At the same time, it is possible for some people to understand it sooner than others. Then, those Beings simply bring the energy back and replay the same moment over and over again, only differently each time. Understanding ascension is to hear the telling of the story. It is not actually a process; it is the sharing of excitement about what has happened to some members of a group that inspires the rest of the group to create the same experience.

It is still so difficult not to get into the linear portion of it. Is that going to get easier?

Yes, it is going to get easier. Remember that the hard part is over. Each time anyone considers all of his or her choices, then makes a decision, and maybe even changes his or her mind and chooses another direction, it changes the matrix that you are all tapped in to. Every time that a single Being makes a choice, or considers a choice, or moves away from a choice, it changes all the possibilities that are available to you and gives you the opportunity to re-choose. If you consider how many Beings are on the planet at this time and how many Beings are making choices, it is no wonder that things seem to change from one minute to the next. Indeed, that is what is truly happening! That is why we said it is so amazing that you can be in your physical bodies during this transition. Just try to comprehend the amount of information you are dealing with on a second-by-second basis, and then remember that it is going to get easier. Once the matrix crystallizes, everything is not going to be as shifty, and you will not feel as uncertain so much of the time.

We want you to notice how well you are all doing. None of you have recently been locked up for being insane. No one has been tortured or killed. If you hear nothing else today, hear that you are okay. Hear that you are safe. You have done it. Go ahead. Heave a collective sigh of relief. Then, watch as everything plays out over the next few months. It is going to be delightful. It is already delightful. It has all been okay for a while now. Find the part of you that can believe that to be true. Look deeply, it is there. This is not to say that there is not going to be emotion and frustration, and that some of the symptoms you have been experiencing won't continue, but they are not going to be as intense. They are not going to occur as often, and they are not going to last as long. You will still experience the need for more sleep a lot as the matrix stabilizes in early 2003. Once that happens, you are going to begin gaining energy, momentum and clarity. There is nothing to do at this point other than to watch as it all settles, and notice what comes through you. The work is done. You have done it.

Can you talk about this idea of physical immortality and using the physical body? Is that ascension?

Once you are aware that you recreate your physicality in every moment, you can recreate yourself however you want to appear at any moment. For example, you can change your age. You can be one hundred and five one second and then two the next second. You are able to do this because you can go back and play moments in time over and over again, changing your physicality in each moment. Each time you go back, you can play out all the different ways that things can happen. You are willing to consider that there are other realities you can participate in, but you assume that there is one true reality from which all other realities are based. Stop giving so much emphasis to one version of reality being more real than any other version. Realize that anything you can envision is equally real—it is just not manifest. Don't confuse creation with manifestation.

Let's play with this idea. Imagine a reality other that what you perceive to be your current reality. Notice that your new reality is directly related to what you want more or less of in your current reality. That is fine. Just notice how logical it is. Next, consider the possibility that the new reality is the true reality, and the reality that you are calling real is not. Then, if you want to take it a step further, envision another reality based on the new reality, instead of on your current reality. Now, you are getting closer to what you are capable of creating. As long as you are focused only on this current reality, you are missing out on all kinds of other possible ways of experiencing yourself. Remember, this is not real. Maybe you can find a new name for it. The unreality? The fake reality?

As an example, imagine a reality with no war. What would all these people in the Middle East be doing if they were not at war? If they were not throwing rocks at each other, they would have much free time. They would not have to go to all those secret meetings or make all those plans. What might they be doing instead? Play with those ideas for a while. Then, take this imaginary world without war, and consider the possibilities that might exist in this world that you have envisioned. Imagine a world without war where everyone could fly at will. Do you see what we mean? There are no limits to what you can create.

The way you are doing it now is basing everything that is changing, and everything that we are moving into, on how you are in the present. In essence, you are basing everything that you are moving into on something that is not real. Now, does that make any sense? You might as well start basing everything you are moving into on practically anything other than this. In earlier sessions, we talked about how, in geometry, there are theorems on which everything is based. Stop using this present reality as the base theorem.

Can we back up just a little bit?

We can relive this moment as many times as you want to.

When I create my reality, can others come to play in the reality that I am creating?

Others must come to play in your reality, because you cannot envision a reality in which you are alone. Let's play with this concept. Even if you did envision a reality where you were the only person on the planet, you could be the only person only in the context of the absence of other people. So, you would need everyone else to leave. There is no way you could create a reality without other Beings in it. It is impossible. You are not the individual that you think you are. You cannot be. You could try as hard as you would ever want to, but it would always be in contrast or in comparison to something else. Even if you were the only person on Earth, the scenario would still include you and Earth.

So, regarding those Beings that still want to create war and chaos and all of that, are we going to have to stay and be a part of their reality?

No. Remember, we have said in earlier sessions that realities are separating out. That is what we meant by there being a piece of heaven on Earth in the midst of war. Those activities are going on in the same time/space moment. You could be in the Middle East and in a piece of heaven, while physically being in the middle of war, and not be touched. You will also not affect the war thought form by being there. Your light will not affect the darkness, and the darkness will not affect your light. You can both be there at the same time and not affect each other. It is rather an abstract concept.

We have talked about becoming apathetic toward all the things that are going on, and I am finding that, with all the things that are taking place around the world, I am not drawn into much of it. I choose not to participate in it.

And they are doing just fine without you!

Yes, but we have been taught to want to help others and to save them and to send our light to where there is darkness. At this point, am I still supposed to send my light and to help the darkness? Or am I simply supposed to stand back, and let it all play out?

You want to send your energy into that illusion of reality only if you want to support the idea that they need help. If you want to do that, go right ahead. Let's look at it another way. We have said that anything in your awareness is part of your reality. That means you are contributing to its existence in some way. Whenever we say that, the next questions you have are: "What part am I responsible for? What part do I play in it? How am I contributing to it? How can I change it? How can I make it any different?" Once you recognize that everything you are aware of is part of your reality, try not to go to that place of responsibility and trying to decide what is yours to do. Instead, simply notice how well you are playing your part. There is nothing to do at that point; just have the awareness.

Am I to honor those Beings who choose to create whatever it is they are creating and to step back and move on to other things?

You do have a part in it, because it is in your awareness at this time, but that is going to change. As the matrix crystallizes and the realities separate out, it is going to be as if realities are within realities, holograms within holograms—but keep in mind, a hologram within another hologram is still an entirely different reality.

Can we be a hologram within the hologram and not know what is happening in the other hologram?

Yes. That is exactly what we were talking about at the beginning of the session when we suggested that you hold in your heart those who are creating war, providing a safe place to play out those thought forms. By holding those Beings in your heart, they can play out their version of reality, and at the same time, not affect your version of reality. That is the hologram within a hologram. When you conceptualize a hologram, you envision it as a third-dimensional sphere, and you assume that everything within the sphere forms the hologram. In reality, what comprises the hologram is only the surface. Visualize it as a matrix around the Earth that actually defines the reality that is taking place.

It can be compared to the Holodeck from the television series *Star Trek: The Next Generation.* The holodeck is a computer that generates holographic realities. When you first walk into the Holodeck, it is just an empty room. It is only once you specify what you want to happen that the computer generates a virtual reality experience based on your request. If you could see the way a holodeck is intended to work, you would realize that it is only a matrix of energy and that you move around in the circuitry of the matrix to participate in the virtual reality experience. The experience is simply the result of your intention being linked into the circuitry of the computer, creating the illusion of an artificial reality.

If you consider the idea of a holographic sphere inside of a holographic sphere, and realize that the one inside is not affected by the one that encompasses it, and vice-versa, then you will begin to get the idea. Each sphere has its own physical sphereness and its own realities within it. If you think about the Earth, there is actually nothing inside the matrix of the Earth. It is just you moving through all the circuitry around the Earth and imagining that this illusionary reality exists.

The same is true for all of the Beings moving around in other places within the matrix, and there is always the possibility of the two realities interconnecting. It is much like coming to an intersection and being able to choose whether to go left, right or straight ahead. More often than not, you do not choose to go down the war circuit, but choose the ascension circuit, instead. Every once in a while, you might even choose the war circuit, just for the fun of it. Although you usually choose the ascension circuit, that does not mean the war circuit does not exist as an option at a different intersection. Since you are more interested in ascension right now, what you are presently calling reality is just the ascension circuitry within a holographic matrix.

Is the divine plan just to be part of the game?

There is no divine plan. As we keep saying, this third-dimensional reality is purely for the experience. There is nothing to learn. There is nothing to earn. There is nowhere you have to go and nothing you have to do. It is just purely for the experience.

Once the matrix crystallizes, can or will or do we already go into that matrix, and just as we play within the Earth matrix, can we play in that matrix, and then go on?

You are already playing in that matrix, because remember, Earth herself is evolving into a fifth-dimensional Being. She is the fifth-dimensional matrix. Imagine that, initially, there was just one matrix that formulated the Earth experience. Then, over time, another matrix formed within the first matrix. Imagine that the outer matrix, for lack of a better way to say it, contains the fifth-dimensional experience, and the inner matrix contains the third-dimensional experience. Next, imagine the two matrixes separating and moving in different directions.

Do you remember that we said that those still interested in the third-dimensional experience are going to move to another place that looks like Earth, where they can continue playing out their creations of reality? Those Beings will move with the third-dimensional experience matrix, and you will move with the fifth-dimensional matrix. The choice that you made on the September 2002 equinox was which holographic matrix you want to play in for the next ten years. Presently, there are multiple connections between the two matrixes, but as they move in different directions, they are going to have increasingly less—and ultimately no—points of connection with each other. Eventually, each matrix will move into the energy field of a new matrix, where new possibilities of experience will be offered. Then, in time, the two matrixes will become one before splitting out again into separate matrixes. Can you visualize that? The reason everything seems so confusing and so uncertain now is because you are aware of two very different realities. As the matrixes separate out, your reality is going to become the only one that you are consciously aware of, and it will become less confusing. That is what is going to happen in this next ten-year period.

What will be our experience once the matrixes completely separate from each other?

There is going to be a ten-year period moving out of the third dimension. Then, there is going to be another ten- to fifteen-year period moving into the fifth dimension. Time/space does not actually exist in the fifth dimension, but that is a useful way to conceptualize it. What you are experiencing now is the holographic matrixes separating out from each other. As you move into the next ten years, there are going to be fewer connections between the two realities. Then, in 2112, Earth will move inside of a new matrix, which will hold within it the components of realities beyond the fifth-dimensional experience and will allow all kinds of new possibilities to come in.

The next ten years are not about possibilities; they are about playing out realities based upon the choices made until this point. You are going to begin moving away from possibility and potential and begin moving into fully experiencing that which you find most interesting for a while. Then, you will move into possibility and potential again. At that point, you can move into a second-dimensional experience, or you can move into a two-hundredth-dimensional experience. What you call reality is simply the act of moving and shifting matrixes of illusion. Picturing matrix spheres moving in and out of each other is a really useful way to conceptualize it.

I need clarification about when we move into another dimension. Will that be our only reality, and will we not be connected to this dimension?

You are interchanging dimensions and realities.

So, we will have the ability to move back and forth between the realities?

You will have the ability to move back and forth between dimensions. What you are going to lose is the moving back and forth between realities.

Okay, explain that please...

We need to clarify the difference between realities and dimensions. We have been talking about realities separating out. We did not say that dimensions are separating out. We said that you are going to be able to move between dimensions. You are thinking that if you move into the fifth dimension and then back to the third dimension, your reality is going to have shifted or changed, because you moved between dimensions—but there is not a correlation there. Regardless of whether or not you consciously move between dimensions, the matrix is shifting, and your reality is going to change. Your intention creates your reality and the level of consciousness with which you choose to participate during your experience. It is merely one choice within that reality. Let's use this storm that is moving in as an example. You can hear the wind blowing the deck chairs into the side of the house. You can choose whether to focus on the storm outside or on the conversation we are having inside the house.

Now, let's back up a bit. Your current reality begins to shift when the matrixes crystallize. Picture the third-dimensional experience matrix within the fifth-dimensional experience matrix. Imagine that there are many places where the two are interconnected. Now, see those links disappearing one by one. After a while, there will be just a few links between the matrixes; eventually, those too will disappear, and there will no longer be any connection between the two holographic realities. As the connections between the two realities gradually disappear over the next ten years, you will become more focused upon the fifth-dimensional experience and will lose interest in the third dimension. In the following ten years, the fifth-dimensional matrix will move into the orbit of another matrix and will begin to establish connections with the new matrix.

What we are trying to convey to you is the understanding of realities and dimensions being different. Remember, within any reality, all Beings have access to all dimensions. It can be compared to taking a magnifying glass and putting different colored filters on it, such as red, blue or green. Everything would look different depending on which filter you were looking through. The colored filters represent the different dimensional perspectives that can be experienced as an illusion of reality. You can already do this, but you are now working on being able to do it consciously. The matrix shift is happening at the same time that you are becoming aware that you can participate in this experience from different dimensions, but the two are not linked to each other. You have always been able to move between dimensions.

Whether you chose the third-dimensional matrix or the fifth-dimensional matrix, you could participate in either reality from multiple-dimensional perspectives. You are not going to be moving between the third- and fifth-dimensional realities, you are going to be moving between the dimensional experiences of the fifth-dimensional reality. When we talk about you moving between the third and fifth dimension, you imagine you will be participating in the third-dimensional reality matrix that contains the war thought forms, but you are not. You are going to be moving between the third- and fifth-dimensional perspectives of the fifth-dimensional reality matrix in which you are currently participating.

There will also be certain Beings experiencing both third- and fifth-dimensional perspectives within the third-dimensional matrix of reality, because they have chosen a different timeline for their ascension process. The third-dimensional reality matrix will also move into another holographic matrix and create energetic connections with it. In that experience, over time, more light will come in, and all the Beings will be presented with the choice of how consciously they want to ascend. The progression will then continue on in that manner.

It is useful to envision the matrixes being of different sizes. Imagine the third-dimensional matrix as being small, the fifth-dimensional matrix as being middle-sized, and the new holographic matrix as being large. You are currently moving between the small and middle-sized matrixes of holographic realities, but soon you will only move within the middle-sized one. After a while, you are going to move between the middle-sized and large matrixes. Eventually, some of you are going to move fully into the large matrix, only to transfer over from that one to one of even larger size that will encompass smaller matrixes. At that point, you will serve as ascended masters in order to bring the possibility of ascension and awareness to those holographic realities represented by the smaller matrixes.

Is it like different civilizations that are living on Earth today, like those people who live in a tribe in Africa, whose reality of Earth is totally different than Americans', with the wealth and the food and everything that we have?

Yes. Both of those realities are equally real, and both of them are going on at the same time and seemingly having no impact on each other. In reality, however, they do have great influence on each other. As Americans, you are not aware of your connection to them, and they are not aware of you.

Have we already made our choices?

Yes. Everyone here has made his or her choice.

What did we choose? Is it all the same?

The choice that you made was to what extent you want to consciously participate as you move through the ascension process. If you think of ascension as changing form, everyone is changing form at this time, even those who are going to continue experiencing a third-dimensional reality. To answer your question, everyone in this group has chosen to participate in conscious ascension to varying degrees. Because we have had a three-year window, you could have made your choice at any point during those three years. You did choose and re-choose, over and over again. You are all very excited about what is coming, and remember, the interest and the excitement is what generates the next version of reality that you will manifest.

Are you saying that what we are in the process of doing is becoming consciously aware of our ascension? Are there people who are still unconscious at this moment who have chosen to ascend?

Yes. Those Beings will ascend in later waves, because, as we said earlier, the ascension process is eventually going to become easier and less uncomfortable. The last of the waves of Beings that ascend are going to be less conscious of ascension, because they are not as interested in the nitty-gritty parts of the process. It is hard for you to think about, because you, and most of the Beings you know, are change agents between dimensions and realities. That is what you do. So it is hard for you to imagine Beings who are not interested in doing that at this point. There are many Beings who are choosing less-conscious ascension. They are not a significant part of your reality anymore, and because you do not interact with them very often, it is hard for you to understand their perspective. There are many Beings who are little affected by the war and who are not interested in ascension, either. They are simply maintaining a separate reality from both of those extremes. It is a middle-of-the-road, average human experience, which is a very interesting experience of reality in and of itself. These Beings, on an unconscious level, do not mind perpetuating a third-dimensional reality and do not mind populating the fifth dimension. They do not feel strongly one way or the other, and they are not conscious of being involved in this process of change. They are simply enjoying the illusion of the reality in which they are currently participating.

What kind of mindset would choose to continue in the third dimension?

When you separate out from divinity, you have no way of recognizing the pure light that you are until you move into darkness. Once you move into darkness, you can use the contrast to experience yourself at different places along the dark/light continuum. You have already moved into density and back out, so you have already done what the Beings who are still choosing a third-dimensional reality are doing now. It is a matter of timing. You chose to do it in this wave, and they chose to do it at another time. Beings who want to maintain the third-dimensional experience are motivated to do so by the thought forms that they are currently focusing on in their energy fields. These are the same thought forms, which you still carry in your energy field from when you were in a similar place of density, that are interfering with you moving consciously into ascension.

Another way to think about this is to remember that your goal, for a long time, has been to move into density. It can be compared to running really fast in one direction, and even after deciding to go in the other direction, your momentum keeps you going in the first direction longer than you meant to. You need to allow the pendulum of your momentum to change from swinging into density to swinging into ascension and awareness. So, the Beings who are still choosing a third-dimensional reality experience are simply experiencing an aspect of themselves that you have already experienced.

I thought that the decision was going to be about whether I wanted to go into the fifth dimension or to stay in the third dimension.

Choosing to go into the fifth dimension is choosing conscious ascension. In order to move into the fifth dimension, you have to increase the light quotient and the vibration within your energy field. You are choosing the reality in which you want to participate as Earth ascends. All Beings inevitably move into ascension at some point. All the Beings who are choosing to continue a third-dimensional experience of reality are moving toward ascension even as they are moving further into density. You can equate consciousness to light. As your awareness of who you are is increasing, so are the amount of light and the speed of the vibration within your energy field.

So, we could have chosen to remain unconscious and gone through ascension anyway, without the angst?

Yes, and that is what many Beings are doing. But, remember: the hard part is over. We want to call your attention to the storm outside again. It has moved in now, and it is not as intense as it was when it was coming toward us. When the storm was moving in, it was windy and cold. Now that the storm is here, notice how much calmer it is. That can be compared to what the ascension process felt like when it was moving toward you, in contrast to how it feels now that you are in it. Let's move into the meditation...

Imagine yourself traveling through space on a spaceship. Spend some time walking around your spaceship. Notice that the other Beings you encounter seem familiar. Notice you know your way around. You recognize where you are on the spaceship, and you know where your living space is and where it is on the spaceship that you work. Take some time now to get a feel for life on this spaceship...

Now, imagine you are in a meeting that includes all of the Beings on the spaceship. You know that the purpose of this meeting is for everyone to be given the opportunity to make a choice. There can be as many people at this meeting as you imagine would be on this spaceship. It can be less than a hundred, or many thousands; just notice how many there are. You are all sitting in an auditorium, and no one knows what is going to happen. All you know for sure is that the Captain is going to make a big announcement. There have been rumors circulating that there are going to be reassignments. You have heard that some Beings are going to be leaving the spaceship, and there have been a wide range of reactions. There has been fear that some of the Beings who are going to leave do not want to leave. There are Beings who have been waiting for this opportunity, and they cannot wait to go on another spaceship. There are Beings who really don't care one way or the other.

Suddenly, the room becomes completely quiet. The Captain steps onto the stage and announces that each and every one of you is going to get his or her own spaceship. He then instructs you to go back to your living space and design what you want your spaceship to be like. You are given catalogs showing different possibilities and access to computerized spaceship simulators so that you can explore all of the possibilities. You are encouraged to talk to other people and to exchange ideas. You are also told that if you do not want your own spaceship, you can join with someone else and have a spaceship together with them. And if you do not want to go to the trouble of creating a spaceship, because that just seems like too much effort, you can just go to lunch, and one will be built for you.

Now, go back to your living space and design exactly what you want your spaceship to be like. It is okay if you do not know the technical terminology and mathematical equations. You can simply imagine what you want, and the computer instantly calculates whatever information you need to perfect your design. Your spaceship will be built for you. All you have to do is envision it. Know that any resources that you need for this project are completely available to you. Take the next few minutes in this meditation to envision what you want your spaceship to be like...

Earth herself can be thought of as a spaceship. A spaceship does not have to be an enclosed, artificial situation. It can be a star. It can be a galaxy. It can be a planet. It can be an ocean. It can be whatever you want it to be...

As you envision your spaceship, think about what form you want to be in while traveling on this spaceship. Do you want to remain in human form, or do you want to take another form? You don't have to choose just one form. You can have as many as you can imagine.

Imagine that you are now returning to the auditorium and that you have your spaceship plans in hand. You might not remember finalizing them, but you did. If you want to look down to make sure, you can flip through a few pages and see that all the diagrams are there and that you have everything you need. See everyone filing back into the auditorium with his or her plans in hand. At each door of the auditorium, there is a computer into which everyone is feeding his or her spaceship plans. See yourself putting your plans into the computer just inside the door as you enter the auditorium. Feel the energy and excitement from everyone around you as you take your seat.

Watch the Captain come back onto the stage and call your attention to all sides of the auditorium, where there are hundreds or thousands of docking bays lining the walls. You notice that each docking bay has a name above it. You are instructed to go to the docking bay with your name above it. See yourself and everyone around you move to their docking bay.

Once everyone is standing in front of the door with his or her name on it, the Captain announces that each of you is to go through the door that leads onto the new spaceship you have just created. You are told that once you walk through the door, the spaceship you are on right now will cease to exist. You are told that on the count of three, each of you will walk through the door below your name and find a stairway or a pathway or a bridge connecting you to your spaceship.

Visualize opening the door. One...

Imagine stepping out onto the connecting pathway to your new spaceship. Two...

Now close the door behind you. Three...

Know that the spaceship from which you just came ceases to exist. If you want to, go and open the door and look back. Now, walk down your pathway onto your spaceship. Know that this will be your spaceship for as long as it delights you. While you cannot return to the reality that you just left behind, know that you can always, at any time, move to another reality by simply designing a new spaceship.

Walk around this new spaceship. Explore it as you did the last spaceship. Notice that you know where you belong. You know your way around. You know where you spend nights, where you sleep. You know where to go when you are hungry. You know what work there is for you to do. It is as if you have always been on this spaceship. You can feel the memory of the other spaceship fading, but it is okay. It doesn't matter. You have everything you need, and you are not alone. It is a wonderful place to be. Feel the rightness of it.

Think back to the ease of creating this wonderful spaceship that you now occupy. Begin to feel as if you have been on this spaceship forever. Feel the recent memory of having just created it fading slowly from your mind. Feel the memory of the other ship fading, as well. It is okay. You have everything that you need here. You are loved, and you are safe. A distant part of your mind knows that when it is time to make another shift, an equally effortless opportunity will present itself. Take a last look around your spaceship, and when you are ready, come back into this awareness, while maintaining the reality of your spaceship. Know that they are both equally real and unreal at the same time.

Remember, you are not leaving it behind, because you are bringing it with you. Know with your third-dimensional mind that you have already moved into the reality of this new spaceship. Know that the reality that you are clinging to, which feels so real now, does not exist. It is not real; you are simply making it up. You are recalling the memory of it. Notice who you are in this present moment. Notice that the surroundings have changed. When you get home, notice how, at first glance, things seem the same, but know that they are not. You might find some objects just a little bit out of position, or colors might be a little brighter or a little duller than you remember them. Notice that nothing is quite as you remember it.

When you are ready, begin to bring your awareness back into the room. Slowly open your eyes. Remember the feeling that you are feeling right now. Notice the clarity and the knowledge that everything is as it should be. If any other thoughts occur to you from this moment on, just recall this moment, and bring this feeling into that moment. This is it. This is what you have been waiting for. Do not miss this experience by expecting it to come at some point in the future rather than experiencing it as it is already occurring. You are blessed and you are loved.

Access Your Personal Akashic Records

Everyone has the ability to gain access into the Akashic Records. Intuition, knowing hunches or flashes, and our quiet inner guidance is often due to knowledge gained from the Records. However, when we receive information that elicits fear or doubt, we often add, delete, change or filter the information. Doing that tempers or neutralizes the usefulness of the information.

Manifestation of reality begins with intention. Once we form an intention, we have set into motion the manifestation of a new possibility. We are constantly manifesting our reality whether we choose to be consciously aware of it or not. Every thought we have creates a domino effect that resonates far beyond what we see manifest in front of us. Questions asked while in the Records can reveal past and future consequences of choices that we have already made or will make. Sometimes, we become lost within our own illusion of reality and lose sight of what we had originally intended. We can become distracted by a new idea, person or possibility that comes into our awareness, and when we turn our attention in that direction, we often forget about the direction we were moving in before the new opportunity presented itself. This does not mean that we must always stay on our current course; it simply means that it is empowering to consciously choose the direction we wish to move in, as opposed to feeling buffeted about by powers beyond our control.

The past and future of each person is recorded on the divine blueprint that exists for each soul within the Akashic Records. Each of us may hold in our mind a vision of the kind of reality we want to manifest, but as it is for any great structural engineer, in order for the actual creation to be truly brilliant, it is useful to consult the plans occasionally. Just as with a building, where each wall must meld into a corner and everything must be level in order to be structurally sound, all aspects of our reality must be congruent for there to be overall balance and spiritual soundness. Accessing information from the Akashic Records gives us, as the architects of our lives, useful guidance to construct a creation that supports our soul purpose.

Information is gleaned from the Akashic Records through the asking of questions. While in the Records, all knowledge stored there is not immediately available; rather, access to specific information is only granted in response to a question asked. The asking of a question indicates a readiness to integrate the information that comes forth. There is a divine guidance that assists in the asking of questions. While in the Records, people often find themselves asking different questions than they had consciously intended, but the questions that get asked inevitably turn out to reveal the most valuable information for their life in that moment.

The questions asked can be about anything. In daily life, we all constantly ask questions: of friends and family, in the form of prayer, or through journaling. Often, we don't expect an actual answer to the questions that we are asking. Instead, we only hope that some aspect of our lives will change and bring resolution to the issues that plague us. However, when the questioning comes from feeling a lack of personal power and ability to actually change anything, the hoped for changes do not usually occur. While in the Records, answers to questions are received immediately, and are often accompanied by explicit instructions on what can be done to bring resolution to the issue at hand. Inherent in entering the Records is a willingness to accept personal responsibility for the creation of our lives. Choosing to consciously access the Akashic Records is an indication that we are ready to evolve into a higher expression of ourselves.

Questions about spiritual growth, relationships with family and friends, repeating patterns and behaviors, recurring dreams, work and finances can all be addressed while in the Akashic Records. The Records are a recording of a soul's journey since inception, as well as its infinite possibilities into the future. If relevant, past lives may be revealed while in the Records.

Once the reincarnation is recalled and the origin of a problem is known, it is possible to view a situation with new understanding and clarity, which can be used to facilitate change. Questions about the future are not usually answered in the form of a prediction; instead, information is given about which path is most likely to lead in the direction of the future that we want to create.

The reason that the asking of questions is important while in the Records is that we already possess the answers to all of the questions that we have, but because much of the information is multidimensional, it is not easily understood by our third-dimensional mind. With the asking of questions, we are able to cognitively articulate what we seek in such a way that we can receive the answer through our mind. As a result, we are able to more easily integrate it into our daily life in a useful and relevant manner.

The Akashic Records, in and of themselves, are simply an energy in which all that defines us in our current form is held. When we ask questions of the Records, it is as if another part of us—a part other than the one that is asking the questions—knows where to find the answers and instantly retrieves the needed information for us. With this in mind, do not be intimidated by the asking of questions. It is not as if you will withhold pertinent information from yourself simply because you do not ask the right questions. You are essentially having a conversation with yourself, and as such, are in the best of hands: your own.

It is of great importance as we move through the ascension process that we learn to trust ourselves, and a significant piece of developing that trust is to explore and understand the decisions we have made and actions we have taken throughout our earthly experiences. From your current, limited perspective, it may initially appear that your choices were destructive or painful, either for yourself or others. However, upon closer examination, you will find the perfection in all that you are and all that you have ever been.

Know that you always receive immediate answers any time that you ask a question. Sometimes the answer may not be in the form that you were expecting or in a form that you recognize. Therefore, it is important to expand the means you use to receive information to include sound, color, geometrical shapes, and even forms that you cannot yet name. In the past, information received through the Records was encoded and symbolic, but as the veil is becoming thinner, you are now able to interpret the information received within the context of your current understanding of reality. The information of the Records has been hidden within the sanctuary of the mystery schools until the time that enlightenment returned to humanity and divine masters once again walked upon the planet. That time is now, and *you* are the masters.

The goal of working through the meditations in the next chapter is to clear any resistance that you may have to effortlessly accessing accurate information while in the Akashic Records. Any unresolved current or past life can affect the accuracy and clarity with which the information is interpreted. By following the meditations, you will release memories held within your energy field that may interfere with your ability to accurately understand and interpret the information received while in the Akashic Records.

The meditations offer a way for the information to be assimilated without having to go through your third-dimensional mind. The concepts presented are based on the idea that you are more than your third-dimensional experience. Upon initially entering the Records, your mind may become overwhelmed simply because it has been in the habit of operating third-dimensionally. Doing the meditations will allow you to make quantum leaps in your understanding, because you will allow the information accessed to bypass your mind and directly integrate into your creation of reality.

As you work with the information contained within the Akashic Records, you will begin to incorporate the vastness of who you are by recognizing the perfection in all that you have created. From that place of non-judgment, you will be better able to utilize the information offered as you delve into the Akashic Records. As you remove the obstacles that inhibit your ability to interpret and understand Akashic information, you will be able to consciously create a new reality that encompasses the past and the future, as well as an understanding of the inter-connectedness of all consciousness participating in your creation of reality.

As you do the meditations, your DNA will be activated, and you will be able to bring the hidden wisdom held within your cellular memory out of the archives and into the present. It is time to remember how to consciously access the Akashic Records so that you may more completely engage in this time of transition. You cannot fully be of service if you continue to operate under the illusion of forgetfulness, and the Akashic Records hold within them vital experience and knowledge that needs to be incorporated into your consciousness as you reawaken to your true essence and remember who you are.

With the overall objective being to encourage you to recognize your inherent divinity and to claim ownership for the reality that you are creating, you will go into the Akashic Records three different times using three different formats. Each journey into the Akashic Records will offer a unique way of entering into and experiencing the energy of the Records.

This series of meditations is designed to assist you in gradually learning to assimilate the multidimensional aspects of the Akashic Records into your cognitive awareness, which will allow you to consciously incorporate the information contained within the Records into the creation of your everyday reality. You can do all three meditations consecutively or you can do them separately, with as much time between as you feel necessary to assimilate your experience or accommodate your schedule. Once you have moved through these meditations, you will have the tools and the understanding to be able to enter your Akashic Records at any time.

Past Life Meditation

In this meditation, you will recall three past lives that are relevant to learning to read the Akashic Records. You will receive a symbolic representation of each lifetime, as well as an understanding of your purpose during that incarnation.

To prepare for this meditation, it is recommended that you record the following script onto a cassette tape or a CD, choose a time and a place where you won't be disturbed, and have the worksheets for this meditation with you to make notes.

Past Life Meditation

Close your eyes and feel yourself begin to relax. Focus on your breath. Notice how it feels to breathe in and breathe out. Allow your mind to become still.

Move your awareness to your feet. Sense a warm, relaxing sensation move into your toes, back through your arches and into your ankles.

Allow this relaxing sensation to move slowly up through your legs, into your calves, past your knees and into your thighs. Feel all the tension that you are holding in your legs simply dissolve.

Feel your hips and buttocks relax as the relaxation moves up your body into your abdomen and lower back. Take a moment to notice how utterly relaxed your lower body has become.

Allow the sensation of relaxation to continue to move up your back and into your chest. Take a deep breath, and let any concerns or worries that you have dissipate with your out-breath.

Feel your shoulders and neck release all tension as the relaxation moves through them and continues to flow down into your arms, through your elbows, and gently out of your fingertips.

Allow your jaw to relax as the relaxation moves up into your temples and out through the top of your head. You might feel a tingling sensation at the top of your head and in your fingertips as the energy of relaxation moves out of your body, taking with it all stress and tension.

Take a moment to notice how relaxed you have become. Observe how even your breathing is and how heavy your body feels. Let go of any concerns or worries that remain, and allow yourself to relax fully into this experience.

Begin to visualize a place in your mind that feels safe and peaceful. This place can be real or imagined. It is up to you. Simply envision that you are in a place that feels serene and calm. It may be a warm, sunny beach, or maybe a quiet meadow, or it might be a room at home that offers you a refuge from the world. Take a few minutes to enjoy being in this place.

~ *Allow three-minute pause in recording* ~

Allow your attention to be drawn to a path that appears before you, and begin walking along this path. Notice the sensations all around you as you slowly move along the path. Use all of your senses. What is the temperature of the air? Notice what sounds you hear. What does it smell like? What do you see around you?

After a while, you notice that there is a clearing in the distance and that there is a structure there. Look for the path that leads to this clearing, move off of the path that you are already on, and begin walking toward this structure.

Find the entrance to the structure and go in. You find that you are able to enter effortlessly. Once inside, you find yourself in the center of a long hallway that extends away from you to your right and to your left, and you are unable to perceive either end from where you stand.

Choose a direction and begin moving down this hallway. Notice that there are doors lining both sides of the hallway as you walk along, and as you look more closely, you recognize that there is a symbol on each door. Take a few minutes and explore the hallway. Stop and look at the symbols on some of the doors. Some of them will be recognizable to you, and others will be unfamiliar.

~ *Allow three-minute pause in recording* ~

It is time to choose a door that you would like to enter. You can either choose a door that you have already passed, or continue down the hallway until you find a door that draws your attention. Once you choose a door, take a minute to observe the symbol on the door before you open it.

Now, open the door and step inside. As you close the door behind you, it disappears, and you find yourself someplace very different than the hallway that you have just come from. Notice what is around you.

Get a sense of the form that you are in for this experience. Begin with your feet, if you have feet. If you don't have feet, simply take note of what is where feet would be, and become aware of what is there instead. If you do have feet, notice what you are wearing on them, if anything.

Continue to observe yourself. Are you in human form? Are you wearing clothing? If you are not human, what do you look like? What shape are you? What color? Do you have a form, or are you simply energy in this experience?

Call to your awareness a significant experience early on in this lifetime, and feel, sense or see the scene around you change. Notice what you are doing. Get a sense of what your part is in whatever is going on. Notice if there is anyone else around and what their purpose seems to be. What are they doing? Does there seem to be any conflict taking place? What emotions do you feel?

If you would like to have more of a sense of where you are, you can ask someone, or look for a newspaper or a calendar or some other type of document to give you some insight into when and where you are. You can also notice what kind of currency is being exchanged or what kinds of food are being eaten. How are people dressed? It may be that none of these details are relevant. It is up to you. Engage with this experience in whichever ways feel most appropriate for you. It is your experience.

~ *Allow three-minute pause in recording* ~

Now, call to your awareness a significant experience toward the middle of this lifetime, and feel, sense or see the scene around you change and, as before, observe what is happening.

~ *Allow three-minute pause in recording* ~

Now, call to your awareness a significant experience toward the end of this lifetime, and feel, sense or see the scene around you change and, once again, become aware of what is happening.

~ *Allow three-minute pause in recording* ~

It is time to move to the moment at which you died in this lifetime, if you are not there already. Know that if the experience is at all painful or uncomfortable, you can observe what is happening as if from a distance. Know that you are safe and that what is taking place cannot harm you. You are simply recalling the experience.

~ *Allow three-minute pause in recording* ~

Observe your energy moving slowly out of the form that you were in during this lifetime. As your essence rises up and out of form, notice that a gentle, loving Being has appeared before you. Ask the Being what your purpose was in this lifetime and whether you were able to achieve that purpose. See, sense, feel or hear the answer.

This Being gives you a gift. It may be something tangible, or it may be an insight, a color, a tone or vibration, a geometrical shape, or something else entirely.

Accept the gift.

Once you accept the gift, you immediately find yourself on the inside of the door that you came through into this experience. Open the door, step back out into the hallway, and as you close the door behind you, take one last look at the symbol on the door.

When you are ready, open your eyes and make notes about this experience on the first past life worksheet. It is not necessary to think of any questions, as you will have time for that later, but if any come to you, write them on the worksheet.

~ Stop the playback of the recording to make notes, and begin again when you are ready to continue ~

Close your eyes and once again visualize your peaceful place. Notice that the same path appears as before, and begin moving along the path. Experience the path using all of your senses.

After a while, you come to the same clearing with the now-familiar structure. Move onto the path leading to the entrance of the structure, and as you enter, you are again in the long hallway. Decide which direction you would like to explore this time, and begin moving in the direction that you choose.

~ Allow three-minute pause in recording ~

It is time to choose a door that you would like to enter. As before, you can either choose a door that you have already passed, or continue down the hallway until you find a door that draws your attention. Take a minute to observe the symbol on the door that you have chosen before you open it.

Now, open the door and step inside. As you close the door behind you, it disappears as before, and you find yourself someplace very different than the hallway that you have just come from. Notice what is around you and get a sense of the form that you are in for this experience.

Now, call to your awareness a significant experience early on in this lifetime, and feel, sense or see the scene around you change, and observe what is happening.

~ *Allow three-minute pause in recording* ~

Now, call to your awareness a significant experience toward the middle of this lifetime, and feel, sense or see the scene around you change, and observe what is happening.

~ *Allow three-minute pause in recording* ~

Now, call to your awareness a significant experience toward the end of this lifetime, and feel, sense or see the scene around you change and, once again, become aware of what is happening.

~ *Allow three-minute pause in recording* ~

It is time to move to the moment at which you died in this lifetime, if you are not there already. Know that if the experience is at all painful or uncomfortable, you can observe what is happening as if from a distance. Know that you are safe, and that what is taking place cannot harm you. You are simply recalling the experience.

~ *Allow three-minute pause in recording* ~

Observe your energy moving slowly out of the form that you were in during this lifetime. Sense that the gentle, loving Being has appeared before you, and ask about your purpose in this lifetime. See, sense, feel or hear the answer.

You are given a gift.

Accept the gift.

Once you accept the gift, you immediately find yourself on the inside of the door that you came through into this experience. Open the door, step back out into the hallway, and as you close the door behind you, take one last look at the symbol on the door.

When you are ready, open your eyes and make notes about this experience on the second past life worksheet.

~ Stop the playback of the recording to make notes, and begin again when you are ready to continue ~

Close your eyes and, once again, visualize your peaceful place. Notice that the same path as before appears, and begin moving along the path. When you come to the path that leads into the clearing where the structure resides, follow it and go inside.

You may find that you have entered at the same place as before, or you may find yourself in a different part of the hallway. Before you decide which direction you would like to explore, take a minute to notice if anything has changed. There may be more options this time. As you choose which direction to go, know that you can quickly bypass any doors that you have already seen if you so desire.

~ Allow three-minute pause in recording ~

It is time to choose a door that you would like to enter. Take a minute to observe the symbol on the door that you have chosen before you open it. Now, open the door and step inside, and as you close the door behind you, as before, it disappears, and you find yourself in an entirely different experience. Notice what is around you.

Get a sense of the form that you are in for this experience. Allow for the possibility that your appearance may be less recognizable this time and that you may or may not be in a form that is familiar.

Now, call to your awareness a significant experience early on in this lifetime, and feel, sense or see the scene around you change, and observe what is happening. If you do not have a sense of linear time in this experience, simply allow a significant moment to form around you.

~ *Allow three-minute pause in recording* ~

Now, call to your awareness another significant experience during this lifetime, and feel, sense or see the scene around you change, and observe what is happening.

~ *Allow three-minute pause in recording* ~

Now, call to your awareness a different meaningful experience during this lifetime, and once again feel, sense or see the scene around you change.

~ *Allow three-minute pause in recording* ~

As you move to a final memory in this experience, you may find that your essence does not leave in the same manner as before. If that happens, get a sense of why it is different than the other lifetimes that you have remembered. Sense that the gentle, loving Being has appeared before you, and ask about your purpose in this lifetime. See, sense, feel or hear the answer.

You are given a gift.

Accept the gift.

Once you accept the gift, you immediately find yourself on the inside of the door that you came through into this experience. Open the door, step back out into the hallway, and as you close the door behind you, take one last look at the symbol on the door.

Allow yourself to move back down the hallway, through the entrance and onto the path leading into the clearing. Follow this path to where it intersects with the original path that brought you here, and follow that path back to your peaceful place.

When you are ready, open your eyes and make notes about this experience on the third past life worksheet.

~ *Stop the playback of the recording* ~

In preparation for the Meeting the Guardians of the Halls of Records meditation, write down at least three questions about each lifetime that has been revealed to you during this meditation in the space provided on each past life worksheet.

Past Life Meditation Worksheet #1

Symbol on door ____

____

____

____

General description ____

____

____

____

Life purpose____

____

____

____

Gift____

____

____

____

Question #1____

____

Answer____

____

____

____

Question #2____

____

Answer____

____

____

____

Question #3____

____

Answer____

____

____

____

Past Life Meditation Worksheet #2

Symbol on door ____

____

____

____

General description ____________________________________

____

____

____

Life purpose____

____

____

____

Gift____

____

____

____

Question #1______________________________

____

Answer______________________________

____

____

____

Question #2______________________________

____

Answer______________________________

____

____

____

Question #3______________________________

____

Answer______________________________

____

____

____

Past Life Meditation Worksheet #3

Symbol on door ____

____

____

____

General description ____

____

____

____

Life purpose____

____

____

____

Gift____

____

____

____

Question #1____

____

Answer____

____

____

____

Question #2____

____

Answer____

____

____

____

Question #3____

____

Answer____

____

____

____

The Halls of Records Meditation

In this meditation, you will meet the guardians of the Halls of Records and have the opportunity to explore the Halls themselves. You will also access your personal Akashic Records and ask questions about each of the past lives recalled in the first meditation.

To prepare for this meditation, it is recommended that you write down at least three questions about each lifetime revealed to you in the Past Life Meditation on the worksheet provided, record the following script onto a cassette tape or a CD, choose a time and a place where you won't be disturbed, and have the worksheets for this meditation with you to make notes.

Meeting the Guardians Meditation

Close your eyes and allow yourself to begin to relax. Focus on your breath. Notice how it feels to breathe in and breathe out. Allow your mind to become still.

Move your awareness to your feet. Sense a warm, relaxing sensation move into your toes, back through your arches and into your ankles.

Allow this relaxing sensation to move slowly up through your legs, into your calves, past your knees and into your thighs. Feel all the tension that you are holding in your legs simply dissolve. Feel your hips and buttocks relax as the relaxation moves up your body into your abdomen and lower back. Now take a moment to notice how utterly relaxed your lower body has become.

Allow the sensation of relaxation to continue to move up your back and into your chest. Take a deep breath, and let any concerns or worries that you have dissipate with your out-breath.

Feel your shoulders and neck release all tension as the relaxation moves through them and continues to flow down into your arms, through your elbows and gently out of your fingertips.

Allow your jaw to relax as the relaxation moves up into your temples and out through the top of your head. You might feel a tingling sensation at the top of your head and in your fingertips as the energy of relaxation moves out of your body, taking with it all stress and tension.

Take a moment to notice how relaxed you have become. Observe how even your breathing is and how heavy your body feels. Let go of any concerns or worries that remain, and allow yourself to relax fully into this experience.

Now, visualize a place in your mind that feels safe and peaceful. This place can be real or imagined. It is up to you. It may be a warm, sunny beach or maybe a quiet meadow. It might be a room at home that offers you a refuge from the world. Simply envision that you are in a place that feels serene and calm.

Take a few minutes now to enjoy being in this place.

Now, allow your attention to be drawn to a path that appears before you, and begin walking along this path. Notice the sensations all around you as you slowly move along the path. Use all of your senses. Notice what sounds you hear. What does it smell like? What can you see?

As you move along the path, your attention is drawn to the path that led to the structure that you entered for the past life meditation; simply notice it and continue on. Down the path a little farther is another path that leads to a different structure. This structure is magnificent, and you instantly recognize it as the Halls of Records.

Now, move onto the path that leads to the entrance to this structure and notice that there are guardians standing on either side of the doorway. Take a minute now and look carefully at the guardians. They may or may not be human. Do you recognize them? Do they recognize you? Do they acknowledge you or do they wait for you to acknowledge them first?

It is now time to ask permission from the guardians to move through the entrance into The Halls of Records. As you address the guardians, do so in the following manner:

- *State your name, for you are highly regarded in this place, and your identity will be instantly recognized by the vibrational encoding within your name.*
- *Announce your purpose for entering into the Halls of Records at this time. This announcement can be as simple as that you wish to Remember Who You Are, or whatever comes to mind.*
- *Ask permission to enter, and know, without a doubt, that the guardians recognize your divine right to enter into The Halls of Records at this time, and they immediately and reverently grant you entrance. See, sense or feel the doors open before you.*

Now move through the doors into the Great Halls and take a few minutes to explore. What does it look like to you? Does it feel familiar? If it feels at all overwhelming, simply begin to focus on details, as opposed to trying to take it all in at once. Notice where you are standing and what is just in front of you, and move forward to look at it more closely.

Get a sense of how information is accessed in this place. Is there one big book in the center of the room or are there shelves or rooms of books? Are there scrolls, screens or something else entirely? How do you move to other rooms within the Halls? Are there staircases, hallways, escalators, elevators or pillars of light? What effects do the thoughts that you have while in these

Great Halls have on your experience? Do they transform the scene around you? Do they move you around within the Halls? Are there other Beings there? If so, what are they doing? Can you communicate with them?

If you still feel overwhelmed, ask Thoth for assistance, and he will appear instantly at your side. You can ask him to answer any questions that you might have, or simply to show you around and explain how things work. Take a few more minutes now to explore this wondrous place.

~ Allow five-minute pause in recording ~

It is now time for you to seek out your personal Akashic Records. If you know where they are, go to them now. If you are not sure where they are, ask Thoth to take you to them. If you are not sure how to access information from them, ask Thoth for assistance.

Once you find your personal Records, you can begin asking the questions that you have written down from your first past life memory, and record the answers that you receive on the worksheet. You are not limited to the three questions that you have written down. You can ask as many questions as you choose.

~ Allow five-minute pause in recording ~

It is now time to begin asking the questions that you have written down from your second past life memory, and record the answers that you receive on the worksheet.

~ Allow five-minute pause in recording ~

It is now time to begin asking the questions that you have written down from your third past life memory, and record the answers that you receive on the worksheet.

~ Allow five-minute pause in recording ~

Once you have asked all of your questions and recorded the answers, see, sense or feel yourself go back out through the entrance of the Halls of Records, and follow the path back to your peaceful place. When you are ready, open your eyes.

~ Stop the playback of the recording ~

Invocations to Open the Akashic Records

Information is acquired from the Akasha through the asking of questions. While in the Akashic Records, all knowledge stored there is not immediately available; rather, access to specific information is only granted in response to a question asked. The asking of a question indicates the readiness of an individual to integrate the information that comes forth.

You already possess the answers to all of the questions that you have, but much of the information is multidimensional and, as such, is not easily understood by your third-dimensional mind. With the asking of questions, you are able to cognitively articulate what it is you seek in such a way that you can receive the answer through your logical understanding. As a result, you are able to more easily integrate the information into your daily life in a useful and relevant manner.

In this meditation, you will use one of the invocations beginning on page 198 to enter the Akashic Records and ask questions about your current life. During this time, you will address any issues or concerns that you have in regard to your current life, as well as any questions about future probabilities and possibilities.

It is recommended that before you do this meditation, you read *Preparing Useful Questions* and *Reading Guidelines* below. To prepare for this meditation, write down at least three questions about your current life on the worksheet provided, choose a time and a place where you won't be disturbed, and have the worksheets for this meditation with you to record the answers received.

Preparing Useful Questions

When you ask general questions, expect general answers. For more detailed information, ask specific questions. For example:

General: Why am I so unhappy?

Specific: Why am I unhappy in my relationship with _______?

What is my job so unsatisfying?

What can I do to be more creative?

What would make me want to enthusiastically get up each morning?

It is useful to address all issues that are affecting your current life from past, present and future perspectives. For example:

Current: Why don't I have any money?

Past: Are there any past life issues that relate to my lack of money?

Present: What current belief systems do I have that interfere with having more money?

Future: What can I do to allow more financial energy into my reality?

Ask one question at a time and listen for the answer before asking a related question rather than asking multiple questions at once. For example:

Multiple: When and where will I be moving and how will I be able to afford it?

Single: When will I be moving?

Where will I be moving?

Where will the money for my move come from?

When asking questions about the future, use the if-then format. For example:

If I want to ______, what can I do now to move in that direction?

If I ______, will that allow/support/assist me to ______?

You will be unable to access information from the Records of others. You can still ask questions about other people, just know that any information offered will be according to what is accessible through your Records. For example:

Not in your Records: Why does ______ have cancer?

In your Records: Is there anything for me to do to assist ______ in regaining his/her health?

At the end of each session, always allow for questions unasked to be answered. For example:

Is there anything else that I need to know at this time?

Is there anything that I haven't asked that would be useful for me to know?

Reading Guidelines

- Make a list of questions prior to opening your Records.
- Give yourself an opportunity to get used to the process by initially asking lighter questions.
- Do not consume any drugs or alcohol for twenty-four hours prior to your reading.
- Avoid consumption of caffeine for two hours prior to the session.
- Drink plenty of water prior to, during, and following a reading.
- Be sure to have eaten within a reasonable time prior to doing a reading. It takes a lot of energy to fuel this process.
- Say the words to open your Records out loud.
- Trust the process. It is not useful to censor or analyze the information as it is being received.
- Use your imagination.
- Allow the information to enter through all of your senses.
- Don't be limited by third-dimensional possibilities.
- Interact with what is happening rather than trying to make something happen.
- Engage with the information received in the present tense as if it is happening right now.
- Ask yes and no questions, as well as open-ended questions.

- Keep your eyes open during the reading, as you are bringing the information into this time/space moment. You are not going anywhere.

- Try both speaking and writing the questions and information received to determine which method works best for you.

- Record or write down both the questions and information received.

- Be sure to always close the Records at the end of a session.

- Expect information to continue to filter into your consciousness through your dreams and in the form of sudden insights in the days and weeks following a reading.

Current Life Questions Worksheet

Question #1 ____

____

____

____

____

Answer ____

____

____

____

____

____

____

Question #2 ____

____

____

____

____

Answer ____

____

____

____

____

____

____

Question #3 ____

____

____

____

____

Answer ____

____

____

____

____

____

____

Invocations to Open the Akashic Records

You can use any of the meditations given in earlier chapters or the following invocations to access the Akashic Records on your own at any time. Once you become familiar with the energy of the Records, you may find that you are given a personal invocation, prayer or visualization to go into the Records directly from your guidance.

There are infinite methods that can be utilized to gain entrance into the Akashic Records, as each person has a distinctive communication style and a unique way of interacting with his or her personal guidance.

It is important to make a point of closing the Records at the end of each session so that you can become familiar with the distinctive difference of what it feels like when you are consciously in the Records and when you are not.

To Open Your Personal Akashic Records

It is with great honor that I am granted admittance into the Akashic Records of (your name) and receive permission from the guardians of the Halls of Records to access information during this reading. It is with gratitude that we receive enlightenment and insight into the questions asked with clarity and integrity as conveyed through me, and I trust that the information offered will serve and support my highest divine expression on earth at this time. My Records are now open.

To Open the Akashic Records of Another Person

It is with great honor that we are granted admittance into the Akashic Records of (their name) and receive permission from the guardians of the Halls of Records to access information during this reading. We trust that the information offered will serve and support your highest divine expression on earth at this time. It is with gratitude that we receive enlightenment and insight into the questions asked with clarity and integrity as conveyed through me. Your Records are now open.

To Open the Akashic Records of a Topic

It is with great honor that we are granted admittance into the Akashic Records of (the topic) and receive permission from the guardians of the Halls of Records to access information during this reading. We trust that the information offered will serve and support our highest divine expression on earth at this time. It is with gratitude that we receive enlightenment and insight into the questions asked with clarity and integrity as conveyed through me. The Records of (the topic) are now open.

To Close Records

With gratitude for all assistance, the Records are now closed.

Printed in the United States
89370LV00007B/107/A

9 780975 486306